ARCHITECTURAL
ILLUSTRATION & PRESENTATION

RESTON PUBLISHING COMPANY, INC. • **A Prentice-Hall Company** • **RESTON, VIRGINIA**

ARCHITECTURAL ILLUSTRATION & PRESENTATION

H. E. Kuckein

Library of Congress Cataloging in Publication Data

Kuckein, H. Eberhard.
  Architectural illustration and presentation.

  1. Architectural drawing—Technique.   2. Architectural
rendering—Technique.   I. Title.
NA2708.K85   1984   720'.28'4   83-17645
ISBN 0-8359-0323-0

Editorial/production supervision and interior design
by Barbara J. Gardetto

© 1984 by
Reston Publishing Company, Inc.
A Prentice-Hall Company
Reston, Virginia 22090

10 9 8 7 6 5 4 3 2 1

Printed in the United States of America

I dedicate this book to my students—
past, present, and future

CONTENTS

FOREWORD

During the implementation of every project, a point is reached at which the design for a building emerges from the verbal abstraction of the program. It is then that the importance of visualizing the design becomes paramount. Drawings of many kinds, along with models, are used at this stage to explore and test the design and to satisfy the designer's own curiosity about his "creation", and to locate problem areas for adjustment and refinement. When these things are achieved, a particular form of drawing, with overtones of photographic quality, is frequently used to show the building in use in its setting, so that the layman client (or the public) can "see what the building will look like."

This book includes many examples of this kind of illustration and reveals the drawing techniques by which they are made. It is thus an excellent reference for all those designers, draftsmen, and students who need to know "how to" make these drawings. The book is also useful for those who enjoy drawing buildings or simply enjoy looking at these special types of drawings.

Mr. Kuckein is a gifted and accomplished delineator. He brings to this book not only the skills achieved over a long period of production of these kinds of drawings, but also the insight of an experienced architect and designer in selecting the appropriate "presentation" that makes the design intent clear.

Professor Douglas Shadbolt
Director, School of Architecture
University of British Columbia
Vancouver

As you are leafing through this book wondering about its content, you will, I hope, recognize that it is not specifically about the subject of rendering. There is no need to add to the profusion of books that deal quite adequately with the many aspects of this commercial art form.

My objectives are quite different, for I am addressing those who are interested in architectural drawing; that is to say, this book is about the language used to represent elements related to architecture that become not only part of the actual design process but also serve as a means of communication with the day-to-day activities of a studio or design office. In preparing the outline for this book, I based my selection of graphic examples on the assumption that the students reading it might have a wide range of backgrounds and interests. A fundamental comprehension of the laws of perspective, balance, proportion, unity, and harmony is understood. Many fine books on these subjects are available for those who may need basic information on this essential part of design and graphic art. This also applies to aspects of shades and shadows. As you probably already know, well-designed architectural forms produce agreeable shadows regardless of the position of the light source, and when shadows are employed accurately they lend realism. Thus, it is important that students become familiar with this indispensable part of depicting existing or proposed buildings before going on to more sophisticated illustration work.

No book, unless it is encyclopedic in nature, can convey all the details that a designer might encounter. The chief virtue of this book as an instructional tool lies in its step-by-step progression from putting to paper the most elementary tones and textures with a pencil to the colored presentation drawings in the form in which I present proposed projects to my clients as an architect. The distorted and fruitless efforts of many who attempt to draw without a fundamental understanding of certain principles can be avoided through diligent study of the lessons presented here, which will help the reader acquire a kind of vocabulary, or a range of language with which to work.

Students in architectural schools and technical colleges find that few of these academic institutions give them the opportunity

PREFACE

to study the subjects of drawing as part of the curriculum, largely because of time limitations. Thus, this subject is frequently ignored. This lamentable situation could be avoided if the student simply set aside a certain amount of time to learn how to draw, progressing as time and talent will allow. Every student of the subject will have an individual objective. Some may desire to become proficient in the joyful and relaxing activity of outdoor sketching, recording objects and events for sheer pleasure. Others may have a more ambitious goal and may wish to acquire a skill that will allow them to produce readily architectural presentation drawings as part of their professional activity.

I have sketched, drawn, rendered, and painted virtually all my life. It is a most fascinating subject to me, and indeed the most joyous moments of my professional life are the precious hours when I can devote myself to designing and graphically recording, in whatever medium, a proposed project for presentation to a client.

Recent years have included teaching architectural design and related graphics to small groups of students and to classes of twenty or more. Invariably, the students' lack of background, as it relates to their drawing ability, restricts and thus inhibits them profoundly as they attempt to record their assigned projects. The information in this book should help to correct that problem.

It is my profound hope that readers of this book will both enjoy it and benefit from it as much as I have delighted in preparing the drawings and text.

H. E. Kuckein

ARCHITECTURAL
ILLUSTRATION & PRESENTATION

PART ONE

Graphite Pencil on Tracing Paper and Illustration Board

As you become proficient in your field of endeavor, you will discover your own favorite materials, and so it should be! However, if you are unfamiliar with materials and have not yet successfully established preferences, you should probably adhere closely to the recommendations made here so that the particular lessons you study will relate to the materials that you will employ. In many instances this relationship is very important.

This chapter is about work with graphite pencils on tracing paper and white illustration board. The money invested in materials at this stage should truly be minimal. Your list will include tracing paper on a roll about the length of your arm; a few good erasers, preferably Pink Pearl (they are less likely to smudge as you erase the errors you are likely to make at this stage); and a good quality mechanical pencil, able to take various thicknesses of graphite leads. You may wish to include other materials at a later stage of your development, but for the purposes of these instructions you will require 2H leads for outline work and for light tones. F, 2B, and perhaps 4B leads produce the deeper tones, even black, and so you must have these on hand, but that's all! Additional grades will merely be a bother and confuse you. A mechanical pencil sharpener will allow you to produce a point on the leads with ease, and a sandpaper block will enable you to sharpen the point of the leads to a chisel-shaped configuration or a conically shaped one.

The drawing surface on which the illustrations in this chapter are based is a smooth illustration board, Hi-Art no. 62. Do not attempt these lessons with a different drawing surface. Your results will be quite different and will only frustrate you unnecessarily. I have drawn on this particular illustration board for years and not once have I had to change to other types. The quality of my drawings suffered every time I attempted it.

For most sketches, the illustration board is cut with a knife to the size required, not larger, perhaps, than the spread of your hand for quick outdoor sketches; these sheets are best supported on a clipboard. An illustration of a building may require one half of a full-size sheet. Beginners tend to use a scale that is much too large. Limit the size of your drawings—you will achieve more agreeable results and will spend less time executing them.

Introduction

The materials mentioned above can be obtained readily in most art supply shops. Discuss your needs with the personnel—you may even meet people there with similar interests. Think of the fun you will have exchanging ideas, perhaps finding someone who will join you on an outdoor sketching trip on a lovely summer's day selected for this potentially joyous event.

You can gather many helpful hints by studying the work of others. Seek out exhibitions, art galleries, and architectural displays as often as you can. Study the drawing style of the masters of architecture. This activity is an indispensable part of your learning process, whether you are a beginner or an accomplished artist or architect. You may be confused at first by all the individual styles you see. Through great effort these artists have created an idiom unlike any other. The way you draw, too, will ultimately emerge from within yourself. Do not be perplexed. It will not be easy at first, but with patience and diligence, and by studying the lessons in the order in which they are presented, you will develop a measure of competency that will carry you on to greater achievements.

The drawings you produce, whether on tracing paper or illustration board, will frequently have to be reproduced. You should contact a progressive printing company and familiarize yourself with the many possibilities for reproduction. Tracings are usually reproduced simply and economically on the numerous types of printing papers available for this purpose. Each type yields a different effect. Black-and-white and color illustrations on illustration board are reproduced by photographic means. This approach is costly at times but will enable you to retain your originals, as is the case with drawings done on tracing paper. You will soon identify the methods and papers that are most appropriate for each particular circumstance. Experiment with all the papers. You will soon discover your favorites.

One last word: Establish your own portfolio. This can be merely a file folder or an old shoe box, in which you keep for ready reference clippings from discarded magazines and newspapers, brochures, catalogs, and even your own scribbles expressing an idea for future reference recorded on the back of an unpaid bill. Ideally, your portfolio should contain information on everything that you may encounter in your work as an artist, draftsperson, or architect. You should be able to refer to such graphic information quickly. As time passes, you will amass a sizable collection of data. I urge you to start compiling *now*, as you have your first skirmish with lesson number one, which begins on the opposite page.

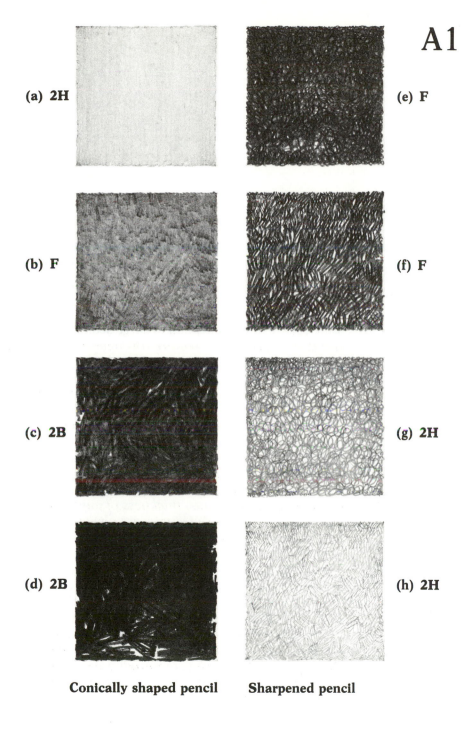

(a) 2H

(b) F

(c) 2B

(d) 2B

(e) F

(f) F

(g) 2H

(h) 2H

Conically shaped pencil

Sharpened pencil

A1

The employment of linear perspective is the most common and simplest method of representing buildings and objects. This approach is often sufficient for preliminary sketches and design studies as it serves to study and establish proportion and other characteristics of a project under consideration. In reality, however, buildings and objects do not exist in outline. They all possess surfaces in a multitude of tones, textures, and patterns, solid or transparent. The tones will vary greatly, depending on the viewer's position, the light source, and its direction. To represent some of these surfaces accurately is the object of this lesson. Working in a black-and-white medium presents special problems in that the texture and tone you create on paper must not only accurately represent the actual surface you are drawing, but it must also create maximum interest. Ultimately, you will want to invent your own way of producing textures, but you should first acquire as much of the skill as possible by doing these exercises. You should do them, as you will readily observe by studying the next illustrations. Beginners need not set out to break well-established precedents. They do need to know the basic principles. The ones here should be adhered to, for they are reliable and are based on many years of experience. Your ability to draw proficiently with a pencil will depend on the amount of time you spend on this basic groundwork. Ultimately, you will discover that by taking the time to do this you will be able to achieve fine results in pencil drawing, whether it be quickly executed design sketches or meticulously prepared architectural presentation drawings. For the exercises illustrated here you will need: illustration board; pencils with 2H, F, 2B, and 4B leads; a means to keep them sharp; and a sandpaper block. Start by roughing in lightly the eight squares shown. Proceed by rubbing a 2H lead at an angle against the sandpaper to produce a conically shaped point. With the flat surface of this point you may now produce a uniform tone on the illustration board [see (a)] with even strokes, each terminating cleanly and sharply. It is important to keep the same value throughout. The darker square (b) is achieved with an F lead, conically shaped, put to the drawing surface with rapid, short strokes in varying directions to produce this somewhat textured panel. In exercises (c) and (d), 2B and 4B leads respectively were used to produce the tones shown. Random strokes, with a dull pencil point and occasional white highlights, produced this effect. Decisive circular movements with an F lead sharpened to a point yielded the effect in (e). The textured panel (f) is produced with an F lead, quite dull, the strokes put down directionally and rapidly. Panel (g) is similar in execution to (e), except that a finely sharpened 2H lead was used to achieve this delicate texture. Finally, panel (h), as in (a), required a 2H lead conically shaped, but the strokes occur at random, multidirectionally.

A2

The beginner often has difficulty indicating brickwork, either on a small or large scale. Many architectural drawings require this material to be indicated. You may attempt to draw the brickwork shown here, but to comprehend the subject properly, you should take a field trip to study materials such as brick. Even better, you should photograph what interests you so you can add the information to your portfolio for future use. At the scale of the brick wall shown here, all pertinent features had to be included: differences in appearance of individual bricks, highlight and shadows of mortar joints, thickness of joints, and the type of bond. These features are obviously most important when they form part of a presentation drawing. Now—draw in carefully all joints with a 2H pencil. With a conically shaped pencil (F), add tone to individual bricks. Proceed by introducing shadow lines here and there with a 2B pencil, taking care to avoid monotony by allowing highlights of the white board to remain. The light source is on the right. Thus a few light diagonal pencil strokes were introduced, where they seemed appropriate, to suggest shadows cast by the branches of a nearby tree.

A3

At the smaller scale, the approach to drawing brickwork is somewhat different because the minute details need not be considered as carefully as in the large scale. Start by drawing the horizontal and vertical joints to scale. Indicate all other features such as the projecting brickwork adjoining the window openings. With a pencil sharpened to a chisel edge, lay down the tones of each brick by running the pencil along a T-square or other drafting instrument you may use. Take care not to obliterate the white highlights as they give sparkle to most drawings. With a soft— perhaps F or 2B pencil—put in the shadows on the receding mortar joints cast by the bricks. The light source is from the right, so that the shadows occur at the bottom of the bricks and on the left side of them. The projecting brickwork near the windows is made lighter to differentiate it from the surrounding bricks. Shadows are introduced wherever required and the sketch study receives a few superimposed diagonal pencil strokes to add life to the drawing, as explained in illustration A2.

A4

Examine some actual stonework outdoors before you try to draw this fascinating building material, with its many variations of tone, color, and texture. You may wish to observe a stonemason at work to obtain an understanding of the material. Observe closely how each stone is cut and chiseled, how the mortar bed is prepared, and how every stone is put into place by a skilled tradesman. The combinations may vary, but each assembly adheres to the basic principles of building with stone. If you wish to represent stone faultlessly in your drawings, study the subject thoroughly by observing as many stone installations as possible; photograph them for your portfolio, and of course make quick pencil sketches. Barring this, you may begin by studying the examples shown in this book, using them as reference material for your work. Keeping in mind the size and type of stone and arrangement of mortar joints, lightly indicate the granite wall illustrated. Having carefully practiced the exercises indicated in illustration A1,

you will now have little difficulty laying down the various tonal values required to make an accurate and visually interesting composition. Note that the direction of pencil strokes is changed from face to face of the stones to give a feeling of reality and to create interest. Deeply receding mortar joints are emphasized with a softer pencil, and dark shadows are made where these would occur. Leave highlights for sparkle. The sense of reality is further heightened by introducing light diagonal shadow lines combined with diagonal lighter tones over the right portion of the sketch, a phenomenon existing in nature where reflective light occurs. Materials such as windows, a garden pond, or shiny leaves after a rain produce these effects. You may achieve them by gently rubbing an eraser over the previously drawn picture to lift off some of the graphite. If you have observed a mason at work and practiced, you will have little difficulty producing fine drawings of stonework for presentation drawings.

A5

Stonework at a smaller scale can be quickly and effectively drawn by employing the suggested exercises accompanying illustration A1. First, sketch the arrangement of the stones lightly, indicating the stone walls projecting on either side of the glazed opening. Lay in tones as you have learned to do so far. Note the contrast created by the shadows. On the stone wall the mortar joints were left lighter so as to delineate them; on the glass a soft pencil produced a deep tone. The projecting stone walls are kept lighter to contrast them with the adjoining surfaces. Occasional dark shadows are introduced in the mortar joints here and there, but spottiness is avoided. The sunlit glass surface is rendered in an even tone of light gray, produced with a hard (2H) conically shaped pencil. The flashing at the top is indicated by the short vertical pencil strokes and is made noticeable mainly by means of the shadows cast on the mortar joints beneath it.

A6

The principles learned so far apply to stonework of any kind. The configuration of this slate or ashlar stonework is once again roughed out lightly, as shown at the right of the sketch. Care was taken to avoid monotony by introducing a variety of stone sizes. A tone of varying intensity completed that part of the work. Deep shadows beneath the stones imply deeply recessed mortar joints. Clean white areas here and there give the drawing sparkle. Diagonally cast shadows lend interest and suggest the direction of falling light.

A7

The stone wall presented here is somewhat more unusual as it is normally quite expensive to build. It generally consists of fairly round field stone broken in half either by subjecting it to heavy blows with a sledge hammer or by heating the stones over an open fire and then allowing cold water to come in contact with them. After such treatment they just crack and fall apart. A stone wall like this is simple to draw yet requires attention to detail. Arranged here are mainly round stones. The spaces between the large ones are filled with smaller ones, just as they would be in actual fact. The faces of the stones receive varying tones of graphite applied with a conically shaped pencil in different directions. To suggest deeply recessed mortar joints, use a soft pencil for the required contrast, which will also have a unifying effect on the drawing. The drawing would otherwise look flat and lifeless—an effect to avoid when including a stone wall in an architectural drawing you plan to submit to your client for approval! Stonework should spring to life in all your sketches. You can make it do so by applying a few strokes to the paper—it's part of the joy of designing and drawing.

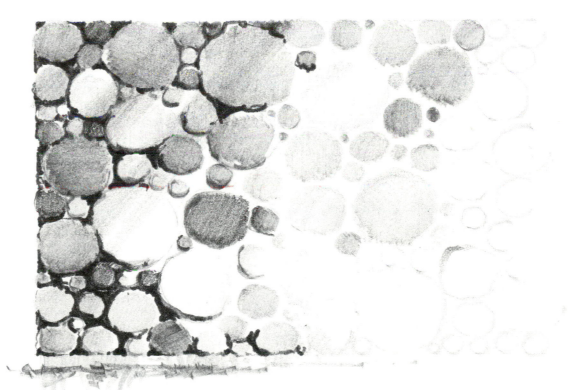

A8

A few sketches of exterior wood facing in elevation are presented here. Since cedar, cypress, or redwood siding is common in many parts of North America, a good knowledge of how to present this building material is of value. Siding—as this material is referred to in building or architectural language—may consist of patterns other than those shown here, but these are the most common three and so we will concentrate on them. All are shown in the context of a roof overhang that will cast a shadow, and so we can study this aspect as well. The drawing at the top shows lapped siding. A medium tone is applied to the boards by vertical strokes with a conically shaped pencil lead. Since boards are normally installed in certain lengths, the sketch is given a feeling of reality when the vertical butt joints are indicated. The portion of the siding in shade produced by the roof overhang is depicted by employing a darker pencil; note, however, that occasional areas here contain light highlights so as not to obliterate the texture of the siding. The extended metal gutter is kept light for contrast. The roof edge is rendered with rapid vertical pencil strokes. The bottom of the siding adjoining the concrete foundation receives an extra dark line to indicate a shadow. The shadows cast by the lapped siding are indicated by drawing somewhat uneven lines with a fairly soft pencil guided by a straight edge. The vertical siding is rendered as described above. In order to differentiate between the varying planes of the board and batten finish in the bottom sketch, you will have to do a little extra work. The raised portion of the wall is simply rendered lighter than the remainder. With the light source on the left, a shadow cast by the batten is indicated to the right of it. The battens in shadow cast by the roof overhang are kept lighter to distinguish them. All three sketches received a few diagonal strokes with a medium pencil to fix the light source and to add interest to them.

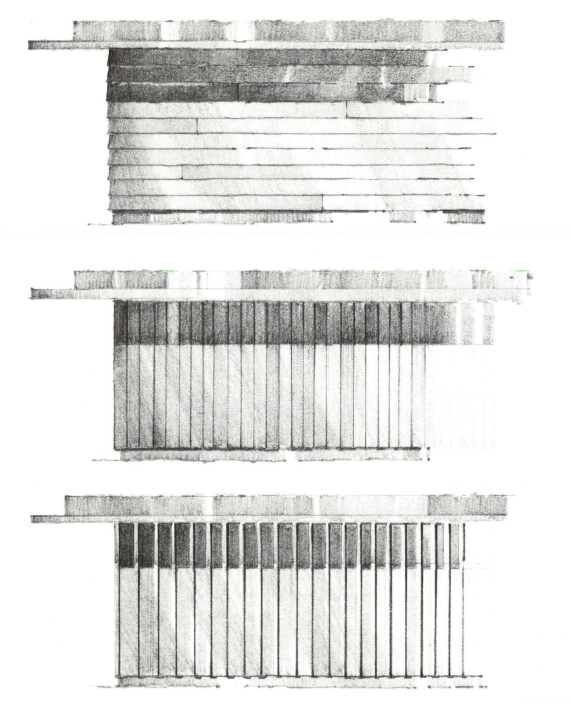

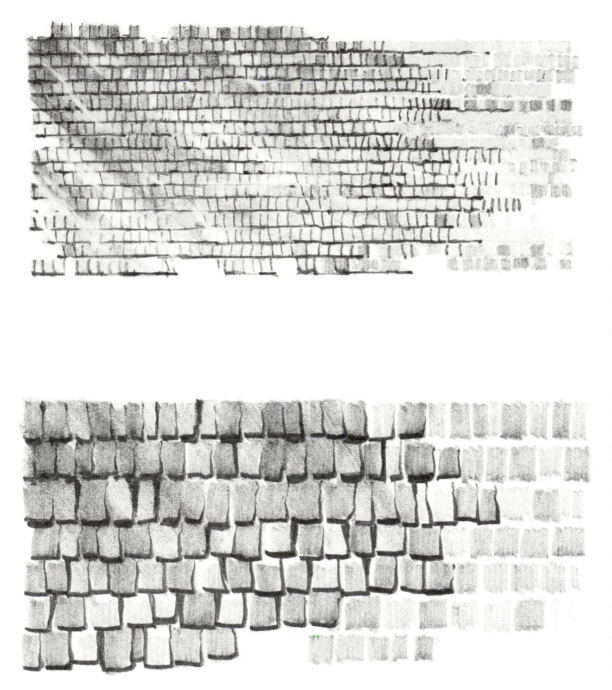

A9

Shingles and shakes, a common roof covering material in North America, will appear in many drawings by architects and designers. As usual, these materials are best understood when studied in actual installations. The sketches included here were produced by laying out lightly the general configuration of the shingles. Employ a straight edge as you attempt this exercise. With a conically shaped pencil, lay down the general tone by paralleling the grain of the shingles. Dark shadows characteristically cast by the upturned butts of the shingles and the spaces between them (and left there by the roofer to allow for expansion) are drawn in to give a sense of reality to the drawing. Avoid stiff and overly straight rows of shingles, for in reality they weather quickly, twist, check, and turn so that a most irregular and interesting texture is the result, even after a short time of exposure to the elements. Highlights achieved by allowing the white surface of the illustration board to show in carefully selected areas are important as they give relief, create interest, and provide sparkle. Without them, a pencil drawing of this kind usually appears lifeless.

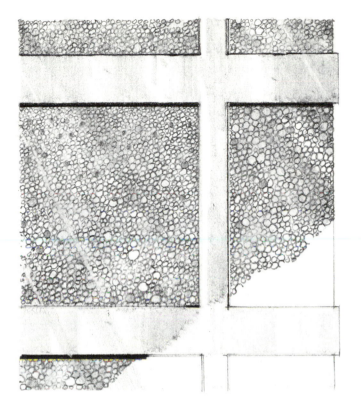

A10

Contemporary architecture involves the use of concrete in a multitude of ways and finishes—singly or in combination. When dealing with this interesting material, try to express the special character it possesses. Concrete is gray, and to depict it with graphite is a simple task. When special finishes are to be represented, you should examine these in detail in order to understand them. You are looking at a portion of a concrete framed wall in which the infill panels consist of coarse, round aggregate, bush hammered after the concrete has set. The general structure is roughed in lightly. The smooth concrete frame is represented by broad strokes applied with a conically shaped pencil. The infill panels are rendered with a pointed one. Deep reveals between concrete frame and infill panels emphasized with a soft pointed pencil and diagonally cast shadows complete the sketch. Allow white highlights to occur here and there.

A11

This differs from illustration A10 in that the textured concrete infill panels are constructed by installing vertical wood ribbing in the formwork prior to the casting of the concrete. After the concrete is set and its forms removed, a certain amount of the projecting parts is knocked off by hand with a hammer. The resulting texture is varied and often multicolored, depending on the type of aggregate thus exposed. A representation of a building so constructed is laid out lightly, as indicated in the bottom right of the sketch. The smooth concrete framework receives a "wash," as described in illustration A10. A gray tone is superimposed on the textured surface. With a soft pencil and set-square, the deep reveals of the fractured surface are indicated by gliding the pencil along the straight edge of the set-square quite unevenly, so as to produce a close facsimile of the original.

A12

You are looking at a detail of an exterior wall panel made of precast concrete. Design studies of this type are often used to ensure desirable results in cladding a building. Simply rough out the general configuration of the panel, including all shades and shadows, and render the entire assembly on the basis of the studies accompanying illustration A1. The glazed surface in shade is produced with a 2B pencil to emphasize this area; when viewed over an entire facade, the depth of the glazing is instantly revealed to the viewer. Joints between panels, often caulked, are indicated with short quick strokes applied at right angles to the direction of the joints. Experiment with other approaches as well in order to find your own way of expressing yourself.

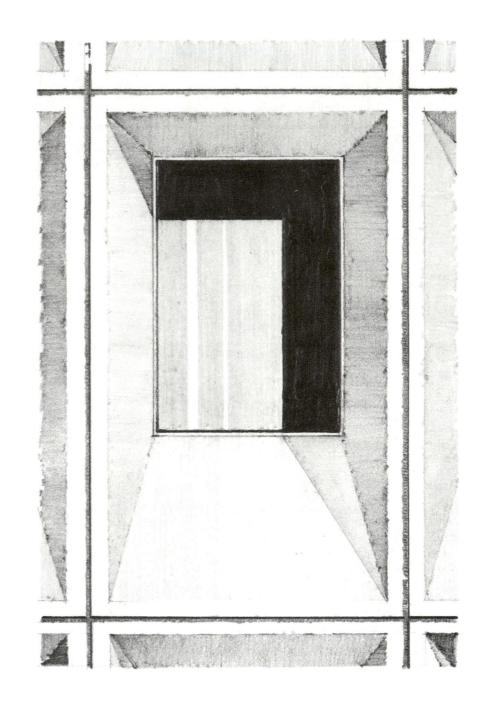

A13

The partly completed facade of the building drawn here is based on illustration A12. It is essentially a horizontal and vertical repetition of what we discussed there. Attention to detail is not as important now, but knowing your subject, how it is constructed and assembled, is a bonus. To this end, study as many actual installations as you can and photograph them for your records. You will gain greatly by doing so.

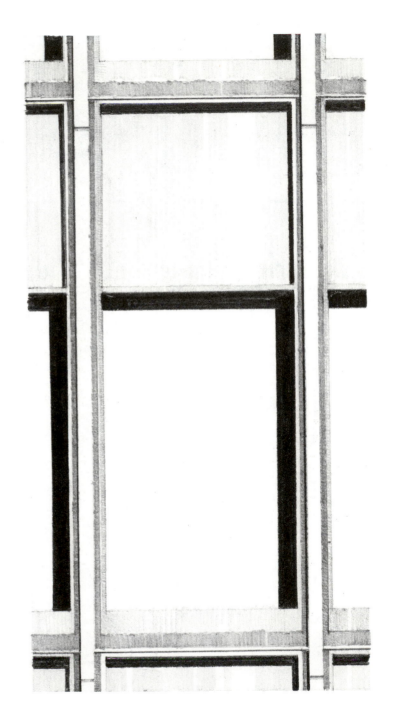

A14

When illustrating a precisely manufactured industrial product such as a metal curtain wall panel, whether in detail or to small scale, you should take special care to transmit this feeling of precision. All elements, shades, and shadows, are considered from this point of view and are drawn in very accurately but lightly. Remember, you are representing a product that has been built to close tolerances. Next, flat "washes" are laid on in appropriate areas with a hard, conically shaped pencil. The glazing receives the greatest emphasis. Draw in very dark shadows and allow them to contrast with the remainder of the glazed surface, which is left white. When rendering an entire building constructed of the above described material, monotony is sometimes the result but it can be avoided, as the next illustration shows.

A15

A portion of a curtain wall facade. This could become uninteresting and downright dull. When faced with that possibility, you may employ several methods to overcome the problem. No need to despair—a building rarely stands by itself. Thus, you may take advantage of numerous objects nearby by allowing them to reflect on the smooth shiny surface of the facade you are rendering. Reflected here is the dark silhouette of an old building giving off smoke from its old heating system. Note carefully that most of the detail from the reflected building has been eliminated in order to avoid confusion. The tone of the reflection is darker on the transparent face and is kept somewhat lighter on the opaque panel. For desirable contrast, allow the vertical mullions to contrast with the dark adjoining surfaces. Diagonal strokes carefully applied or highlights created by lifting off some graphite will add interest. Other details such as clouds, trees, the sun's reflection in the facade, or even distant mountains may play a part in the composition of your rendering singly or in combination. However, start with adjoining buildings. They are convincing. More about reflections later.

A16

We now direct our attention to an aspect of drawing that is a must for anyone involved in these studies—still life sketching. Since a multitude of arrangements are possible, students will gain greatly in terms of composition by doing such studies. You will learn to record quickly and will develop a feeling for the materials used in buildings. A satisfactory rendering with complete entourage will probably be difficult to produce by anyone who has not engaged in some still life sketching similar to the illustration presented here. From a building material supplier or junk yard, collect various items you think appropriate for this purpose. Arrange them so that balance, proportion, and the general composition appears satisfactory. Now, with your total array of pencils, eraser, sandpaper block, and illustration board at hand, proceed to rough in the general outline. This should not take more than a few minutes. If you are satisfied with your effort, proceed by employing appropriate pencils to fill in the areas. It is important that darkly rendered surfaces adjoin light areas and vice versa. Dark shadows are introduced where these might bring an object into focus. Complete a study like the one shown here in less than an hour and undertake many such exercises. They are truly the basis for understanding how to draw.

A18

Materials possessing a highly polished surface, such as the chrome-plated flush valve shown here, require a special approach. Usually what you see is what the object reflects. If you concentrate on that characteristic and use appropriately placed shadows, the results will be acceptable. Try similar exercises with bottles and jars, studying them carefully at first. Draw a portion of the chrome-plated hub cap of your car after you have gained a measure of confidence. The swirling patterns of reflected objects are particularly interesting and will teach you a great deal. This sketch was produced by carefully observing and lightly blocking in all visible configurations. Highlights were defined by applying "washes" in varying tones with a medium hard, conically shaped pencil.

A17

Like the previous sketch, this one is based on a simple brick and an adjustable form insert. The dark background helps to produce the necessary contrast and gives emphasis to the coils of the metal insert, which were left partly white. Once again, conically shaped pencil leads are the basic tool. After a careful outline is drawn with a pointed 2H lead, all forms are rendered with rapid strokes to give this simple subject matter a lively feeling.

A19

*Having settled comfortably on a shady knoll with
an interesting grouping of trees before you, make
a rough outline of what you see. The arrangement
chosen for this exercise will allow you to
experiment with what you have learned so far.
Here we have large pine trees, trunks bare of
branches, against a background of younger
evergreens. Of course take liberties when
arranging your composition. At this stage, you are
trying to learn something about tree structure;
this exercise will spare you the anguish of having
to "render" formless configurations that observers
are expected to identify as trees. Since many
architectural sketches and renderings involve the
representation of different types of trees, you
should become familiar with the most common
tree forms. Photograph trees you encounter in
your travels for your portfolio. But back to our
sketch. You are satisfied, the composition pleases
you, and you are about to begin the final sketch.
One moment, please! Reflect briefly, and firmly
establish in your mind where the dark portions of
the drawing should occur and what you will do
about contrast to give interest to your drawing.
This settled, you will now be ready to start.*

A20

The sketch shown here presents the smaller trees, which are generally quite dark, directly behind the trunks of the large trees. However, small areas of white are allowed to show, and the vertical trunks of the smaller trees are identifiable. Against this dark background, the heavy trunks of the tall pines, which for contrast are left white, occur in the foreground. As these trunks rise toward the white sky, they are rendered in medium tones just as you can see in this drawing. The smaller foreground tree, very dense with foliage, silhouettes strongly against the sky. The light source is on the right; the trunks are thus darker on the left. Diagonal shadows, cast by overhanging branches, are indicated with a hard, broad pencil. The small pines in the extreme distance were produced with a few strokes of a hard, broad pencil. The dead branches in the foreground and the forest floor are drawn as shown. The overall effect is satisfactory and has the required interest. The trees are arranged in balance, and the contrast of light areas against dark surfaces and vice versa prevails throughout.

A21

An arrangement of young pines stands out against a generally light background. This is your introduction to drawing a sky, as well as cloud formations. It is one of the more difficult aspects of the outdoors to render in pencil, particularly when a large area of sky is to be treated. You may begin by sketching in lightly all forms, including the cloud configurations, as they have an effect on the composition. Foreground trees are dominantly silhouetted against a hazy, lightly rendered background. The darker portion of the sky is given a few strokes with a hard, conically shaped pencil to indicate the cloud formations, which will contrast sharply with the areas of the white illustration board occupied by them, if those areas are left untouched.

A22

This grouping of deciduous trees derives its form largely from the intensely dark sky that surrounds it. The light source is presumed to be on the right. The left side of the trees might therefore be in shade, which is indicated with a few precise strokes with a conically shaped pencil. Sketches employing this approach are helpful, particularly when quick sketching is part of the design process, as they put objects readily into focus.

A24

Once again, the principle of contrast is used to define the various tree forms. The trunks and portions of the foliage are sketched in. The sky received a medium dark tone put down with a conically shaped F lead. The distant hill is rendered with a 4B pencil. Against this background, the trunks and branches of the trees are kept white, save for a few dashes with a broad, but hard, pencil. The foreground is only hinted at by means of a few well placed pencil strokes. For contrast, give the lower portions of the tree trunks a few dashes with a soft pencil.

A23

These leafless branches of a grouping of young alders have been sketched against a background of mountains and sky. The tree branches were lightly roughed in beforehand. The composition was completed by locating the remaining features. A sketch of this type relies mainly on contrast. The branches, which are kept white, are defined by rendering the background almost black (use a soft, broad pencil). Against the white sky, the thin and tremulous upward reaching branches are executed in simple broad lines with an F lead pencil that is conically shaped. Rotate the pencil for varying widths of lines. A sketch of this type should not take more than ten minutes. With practice, you may accomplish it in nine or less. In any case, practice this type of sketching as it will enable you to quickly jot down the surroundings accompanying your design work.

A25

The trees emerging from the underbrush of a small forest in this outdoor sketch were the destination of a sketching trip undertaken by a group of students on their first encounter with nature. At first, the subject matter seemed overwhelming because so many things were happening. Light and shade further confused the scene. What to draw? How to sort out the tangled confusion of nature, richly represented? Obviously, this complex subject could not be rendered in minute detail. After investigating numerous vantage points, I chose one that suggested potential. In this type of situation, that is what you must do. Before you start to draw, think hard about what you see before you. In your mind reduce complex subjects to simple terms so they may be committed to paper. In this case, I decided to define the trunk of one large foreground tree, a cluster of trunks belonging to trees nearby, some foliage, underbrush, and the inevitable dark background of a forest. The scene was reduced to these simple elements. A light outline of all the elements described above was put down. The dark background, which is the key to the entire composition for it ties these elements together, was rendered with a broad, black pencil in order to define the subject to be drawn. The trunks of the background trees received a medium tone with broad 2H and F leads. The large trunk in the foreground was "washed" in light gray on its right side, somewhat darker at its base for definition. Without any concern for detail, the general foliage and underbrush were merely hinted at by the application of a few broad bold dashes. Sketching time? One hour and twenty minutes.

A26

Like the previous sketch, the one here was the result of a sketching trip, except that this time the students were more confident. The drawing was executed in less than two hours. Although it possesses no recognizable detail, it successfully represents what was intended. The key is the extreme contrast.

A27

A sketch of jagged rocks and a leafless tree is jotted down for future reference as part of a proposed vacation house. Broad pencil strokes were used to record in minutes a scene that ultimately became part of a presentation drawing. Sketches such as this one are valuable not only in recording actual site configurations but also in conveying a feeling for the site. Such sketches are an indispensable part of the design process.

A28

A lonely arbutus tree covered with foliage is shown here, as is so often the case, clinging to a steep rocky outcropping on the shores of the ocean. Its outline is sketched in. The light source from the right determines the darker tones on the left of the foliage. The principle of setting light against dark and dark against light is fundamental and defines the shapes of branches and the leaf mass. Thus, each is brought into focus and becomes instantly recognizable. A conically shaped pencil with an F lead was used to record this scene in a few minutes.

A29

This brick garden wall was rendered with a chisel-shaped F lead pencil and a straight edge. Mortar joints have been left white. An occasional brick is emphasized either by pressing harder on the chisel-shaped pencil or by going over the same area repeatedly. The foliage of growing climbers is hinted at by showing their shadows. Diagonal dashes over the brick wall fix the direction of the light, and a few additional quick pencil strokes complete the scene.

A30

At times, flowers have to be part of an architectural rendering. Unless you have actually made a few sketch studies of flowers, you may find them difficult to render. I have therefore included one sketch showing how a grouping of lupines may be presented. Frank Lloyd Wright frequently included these lovely flowers in his drawings, no doubt because of the sense of verticality they convey. If a dark background is included, let the flowers form a silhouette against it. With a few additional indications, the character of the plants you are rendering should emerge. Go outdoors and try a few sketches. Even if the results are not as you first expected, the colors and their aroma will delight you. And when you need them, the sketches will be ready to include in your major works!

A31

To render or represent reflections, you must understand a few basic principles. The elevation of a Berm house (see illustration B39) I developed a few years ago consists of large areas of glass facing south. Such a large area could appear dull unless dealt with appropriately. The areas of glass in shade are rendered black with a soft pencil. The clear glass surfaces received a "wash" applied carefully in vertical strokes with a hard, conically shaped pencil. Reflections of trees are drawn with a soft-leaded pencil. For contrast and interest, trees are executed in lighter tone.

A32

A small wooden structure with a deeply sloping roof is sketched here reflected on the surface of a lake. The entire composition was roughed in. Proceeding at the top, the sky to the left of the roof was drawn dark with short vertical strokes to allow the roof and the supporting beam to silhouette lightly against it. To the right, the tone of the sky is light, thus silhouetting the dark beam and roof edge. The background of young pines was quickly sketched in. A stone wall separates the lake from the land mass. Note that this is drawn so as not to appear monotonous. The reflections are similar to the building but are less sharply delineated (the edges are allowed to be fuzzy). Superimposed are short, vertical, broad pencil strokes that allow long, horizontal, somewhat fuzzy, white lines to occur throughout. The smoke emerging from an outdoor fire or barbecue conveys a feeling of tranquility.

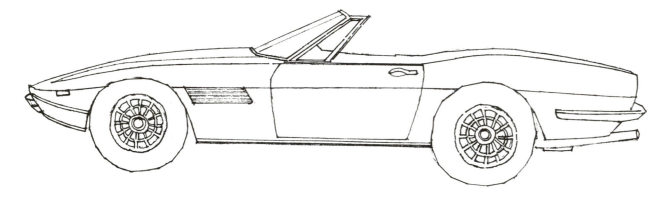

A33

Renderings or even conceptual design sketches often contain automobiles to lend reality as well as "scale." This sketch illustrates how you may go about accomplishing such a task. To draw cars accurately, you will have to go through numerous exercises; do these by referring to manufacturers' catalogs, which you should keep in your portfolio. Remember, however, that the appearance of cars changes with time because new models are introduced. Since classic sports cars are less apt to change, one such car is illustrated here. After studying the characteristics of a car you wish to draw, rough in the outlines with a hard, sharp pencil and straight edge, which is rotated as required to obtain the curves. A French curve may be an alternative aid. After numerous attempts, you will discover just how much detail an outline sketch of this kind should include.

A34

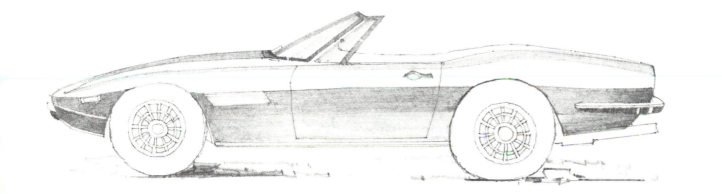

Concentrating on the body of the car, lay down tones of varying intensity with a conically shaped pencil. Use long, decisive strokes, precisely delineating reflections. Chrome work reflecting dark surfaces is rendered with quick strokes at right angles to the direction of the members. Occasionally white highlights of the drawing surface are allowed to break the pattern. The windshield is done with just a few broad strokes.

A35

Render the darkest tones with a soft lead; without such tones, the illustration will look flat and uninteresting. Concentrate on the tires and wheels, delineating them accurately. Finally, put in the complete shadow cast by the car, the texture of which will be determined by the surface on which it occurs.

A36

Photographs of cars that you may have taken yourself and brochures of cars are obviously helpful here as they will provide references from which you can select a suitable model when you need it. Thus you will not be forced to do the required research at a time when you can least afford it. As in the previous lesson, the outline of the vehicle is carefully drawn in, this time in perspective. In so doing, ascertain accurate proportions and then proceed to the next step.

A37

The body is rendered with decisive strokes. Dark reflections convey an impression of sophisticated polish. All work at this stage was executed with a conically shaped F lead, the darker surfaces achieved by going over previously drawn surfaces several times. Reflections on the windshield are indicated. The drawing still lacks interest because there is no contrast. To find out what is required, let's look at the next sketch.

A38

Finally, draw in the deepest tones with a 4B lead. Leave highlights pure white for contrast, where appropriate. Allow the bottom of the car to merge with the road surface visually by fusing the two. Many renderings do not require this exacting detail. However, do become familiar with the subject by observing automobiles outdoors. Study the swirling reflections on the polished metal surfaces, the cast shadows, the way the high sheen of chrome-plated surfaces reflects objects. Look at this sketch again. What makes it an entirely convincing and interesting rendition of a sports car? Aside from its accurate proportions, the high contrast contributes to the success of it. Dark surfaces against light and light surfaces against dark, as has been discussed before, are the key to this kind of drawing.

A39

Figure drawing is not our main concern here, but figures, in all their textural variations, lend scale to architectural drawings and should thus be included whenever appropriate. You may wish to photograph and sketch people as an exercise, or for inclusion in your portfolio. Note how the figures indicated here appear dark for contrast against a white background. Conversely, allow figures against a dark background to be silhouetted in light tones. Men and women—fat and lean, young and old—usually make up the average street scene; become familiar with the varying poses people take and learn to jot these down with a few pencil strokes. When figures are part of an architectural delineation, allow them to blend into the drawing.

A40

Close-ups of the people you draw will require more detail and thus more skill. The same principles apply to distant figures, and in this case be sure to fuse them into the drawing. After all, they are secondary in an architectural illustration and are included only to give scale and lend a sense of reality.

A41

This sketch demonstrates that by applying the principles learned so far you can represent a range of hills with a few strokes. Note the contrast between the various elements. The sky, darker toward the top of the drawing, lighter at the bottom, allows the treed hills to be strongly silhouetted against it. The young pines would be lost in reality. At this point use artistic license and let them silhouette against the darkest portion of the hills by leaving them partly white. The lake in the foreground is drawn with a few horizontal and vertical strokes, and a few highlights are included to suggest reflections. The sky is sketched in with decisive strokes. The time required to complete a sketch of this kind is less than five minutes.

A42

In contrast to the previous sketch, this one shows the snow-covered mountain range silhouetted against a dark sky, and its jagged peaks are thus clearly defined. A few shaded areas are given a medium tone with a conically shaped 2H lead pencil. The foreground, including trees, which is made very dark, is drawn in a minute or less. Once again, it is made to stand out strongly against a white background. Sketches like these are helpful in that they effectively embody the major principles of drawing. Your portfolio should contain numerous such sketches. They are what this book is all about.

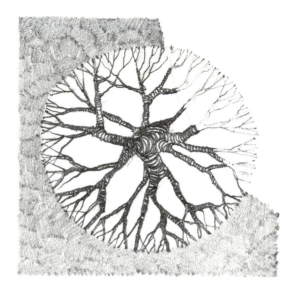

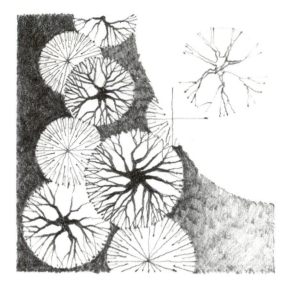

A43   A44   A45

Architectural renderings of site plans often employ symbolic methods and some of the most common ones that I have used in my practice are represented here. The sketches have not been completed so as to indicate how one might rough in the preliminary outline of items to be rendered. Note that contrast is often the key to success in making the various elements instantly recognizable. You should attempt plan elevations similar to the nine squares illustrated. Each speaks for itself and represents landscape materials employed by architects and designers. Finally, after having done these exercises, develop your own symbols. You will need them in architectural presentation work.

A46

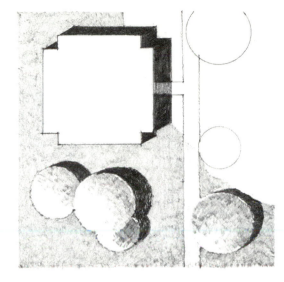

A47

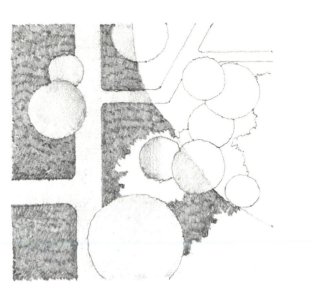

A48

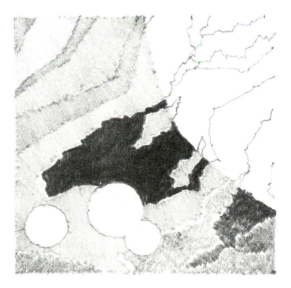

A49

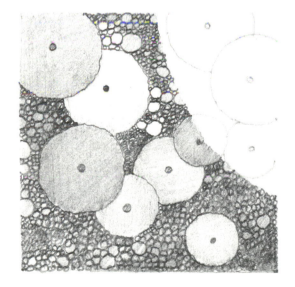

A50

A51

A52

This pencil outline drawing of a town house was the basis for a pencil rendering of an elevation for a project completed a few years ago. Most elements, including location of shadows, are carefully sketched in. A quick value study may be done by laying down tones on tracing paper over the outline drawing to establish the range of values for the rendering. Once this is done and the end result firmly in mind, the execution of the rendering may begin.

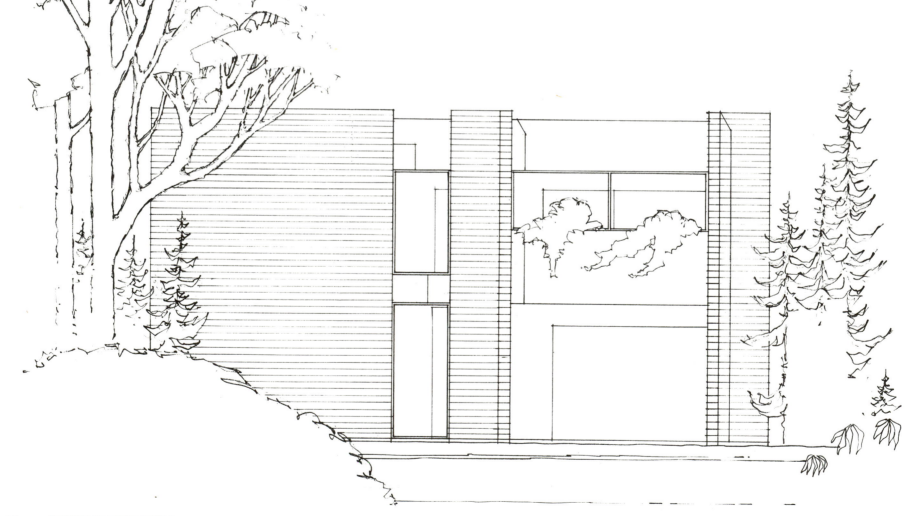

A53

The first step was to draw the varicolored brick walls, which were put down as described earlier. Roof and spandrel panels of plywood received a light tone of gray, but here and there the white background surface was allowed to remain untouched. Trees and shrubbery were put down with special regard for contrast. Broadly drawn road and parking surfaces form a good base. For emphasis, the shadows on the glazing are rendered with a soft black pencil. Figures and the vehicle give scale. The entire drawing is balanced, tones are well distributed, and the overall impression is satisfactory. Sketches of this type will enable you to study the proportion of a project in progress.

A54

In a project calling for the delineation of the partial cityscape of Vancouver, British Columbia, this aerial photograph was the basis for the drawing shown in illustration A57. As is often the case, a photograph is required in order to achieve accurate results for an undertaking of this magnitude. As you study this photograph you will discover that only main features and configurations of the city are discernable, thus additional photographs may be required which are taken from eye level on the spot to record critical assemblies, such as the intricate arrangement of a curtain wall pattern or the lacework of structural steel supporting a bridge. The direction of sunlight will determine shades and shadows. Thus, all photographs must be taken at approximately the same time of day.

A55

Before the actual layout and rendering of the cityscape were undertaken, it became obvious that the value studies included here would determine the method of approach. Large areas of water embrace the major portion of the scene. The buildings could be brought into strong focus visually by rendering them quite dark, in contrast to the water, which was left white. General indications of bridges, main arteries, a wooded park, and a sky for contrast, sketched very dark, completed this preliminary study.

A56

Here the water was treated as a very dark reflecting surface in order to emphasize the major land masses, which were sketched somewhat lighter for contrast. The sky, which was left white here, ultimately included some cloud formations, as shown in illustration A57. No attempt is made at this stage to sketch elements in detail. The purpose of this type of study is to establish tones, contrast, and general massing. Once this is done, one is ready to start the final drawing.

A57

As you study this drawing, you will note that the technique employed to produce it and the presentation drawing of a single building differ considerably. All detail of the individual buildings is eliminated and only major characteristics are focused on to make them identifiable. In an overall view of the city, the buildings become the detail. One of the main concerns is to keep the various elements in the total picture separated so that they will become identifiable to the viewer, more so than they would in a photograph of the same subject. Focus on the main features, and allow them to contrast against adjacent surfaces that are less important. The various tones that were established with the value studies should be strictly adhered to at this stage. A rendering like this takes many hours and you should maintain a uniform tonal value over large areas to ensure that the end result is cohesive. Numerous miscellaneous elements were introduced to provide contrast and to add interest to the drawing. Areas that might be unimportant from an architectural or visual point of view are kept more sketchy and are drawn, without much detail, in neutral tones that contrast with the newer, more contemporary buildings, which, although they lack detail, appear crisp, and clearly identify new development. About half of the work involved laying out all the elements accurately and carefully adhering to the laws of perspective. This was done lightly but firmly with a pointed 2H lead pencil. The remainder of the rendering was executed with pointed and conically shaped lead pencils (F, 2B, and 4B), which allowed the water surfaces to be drawn in with ease. Since the actual method employed is probably a somewhat personal one, the reader may wish to consult the exercises in illustration A1, which form the basis for the many tones and textures in the drawing. Do not be overwhelmed by the complexity of the task. At first, draw only a small portion of your favorite cityscape as an exercise; then enlarge upon this as you gain confidence. An individual style of drawing cannot be taught; it can only develop naturally. I hope that is what is happening to you as your knowledge increases and your technique becomes more your own.

A58

A small portion of the previous rendering is presented at a larger scale here to give a clearer indication of tones, textures, the actual pencil work involved, and of course the inevitable contrast of light surfaces appearing against dark and black surfaces. Whenever possible, leave the pure white of the illustration board untouched for this purpose. Minute details are drawn with pointed pencils. All other work is done with conically shaped leads in varying degrees of hardness, put to the drawing surface with direct, broad strokes.

AERIAL RENDERING OF A CITY (DETAIL)   53

A59

As your ability to draw improves, you may not wish to confine yourself to subjects related to architecture only. Other subjects present a refreshing change, permit you to practice your hand, and allow you to discover other areas that will ultimately be of great value to you. To this end I have included a few such drawings; I executed them for the shear pleasure of drawing them, and so should you! This famous ship, which in 1944 became the first ship to circumnavigate the North American continent, is the focus of our attention now. It was drawn from photographs found in archives depicting the actual ship in the icy waters of the northwest passage. The drawing was produced by carefully sketching in all the elements with drafting instruments. A quick value study that preceded the actual drawing was rendered by the techniques described in previous lessons. The key to this drawing's success lies in the multitude of contrasts achieved through the careful placement of dark areas against light, or even white, surfaces.

A60

These boat repair sheds are based on a photograph taken from a distance with a telephoto lens. Highly contrasting tones make the drawing interesting. The large shed in the rear of the picture is simply silhouetted against a gray sky. This type of interesting subject matter will challenge one's ability. Every city, town, and village provides such challenges through similar types of material, so proceed by doing a few such sketches of your own.

A61

In many respects, this is similar to the previous illustration, but it is composed entirely of elements taken from numerous photographs in my portfolio. You, too, should practice composition by taking elements from varying background material, even your own memories, to compose a visually interesting picture. This exercise will be good training and help you immensely in the task of producing an architectural presentation drawing.

A62

This scene depicts dilapidated old brick buildings facing a lane. They are a most interesting challenge because of their textures. Although the drawing is based on a photograph, many elements have been moved around in order to allow for maximum contrast in this sombre subject matter, which has been kept more or less in a neutral gray in contrast with the foreground building to the left of the picture, which is rendered almost black with a conically shaped 4B pencil lead. Balance is achieved by introducing the wash (pure white for the purposes of this drawing) hanging from a clothesline, which contrasts with the deeper tones of gray of the brick walls. The telephone pole leans slightly; it draws attention to itself and so contributes to the overall balance of the picture. In case you wondered—the bricks were rendered with a chisel 2H and F leads quite unevenly, guided by a T-square held to a vanishing point previously established, and now firmly pegged, in the form of a glass pin! As you set out to do drawings like these, establish all the values you intend to use beforehand. Do not proceed believing that you can erase portions of the drawing you do not find acceptable; that would be a fallacy, for in so doing you would lose much essential sharpness.

A63

Trees again—this time the pruned trunks of typical city trees bear the first fresh branches of new growth, set for interest against a darker sky. Only the bases of the trunks are sketched darkly in contrast to the lighter background of the rooftops of distant houses. Again, contrast is the key to the drawing, which embodies the principles emphasized earlier. The silhouette of the trees was sketched in. The sky was rendered with an F conically shaped pencil fairly uniformly applied with short brisk strokes. The trunks of the trees received varying tones of gray, put down quickly and freely to give form and texture. A nearby street light illuminates this melancholy subject silhouetted against a night sky. Drawn from a photograph taken with a time exposure, this rapidly executed sketch clearly transmits that feeling.

A64

The task of drawing a portion of a wilderness scene filled with distant and near trees highlighted by the sun, and others in deep shade, may be bewildering. Allow your mind to roam. Think of what we have discussed so far. You want to record an impression of the scene, for to depict it exactly would not only require an inordinate amount of time but could probably be achieved more readily by means of photography. Our aim, then, is to establish a criterion—eliminate all detail and differentiate between the various parts, bringing forth the most obvious characteristics of each. If you establish a foreground, a middle ground, and a background, then you can concentrate on these parts. In this drawing, the trees close by are rendered almost black with bold strokes of a conically shaped pencil. The various trees highlighted by the sun in the middle distance are left virtually untouched by the pencil, their configurations silhouetted against a neutral gray background that defines them clearly. The hazy mood is accentuated by the rising morning mist, which obliterates all detail at the base of the trees. Our task is therefore to hint at the profuse underbrush by a few light strokes of the pencil, suggesting only what may lie beyond.

Preliminary work, particularly the plotting of perspectives that is invariably done on tracing paper, is often difficult to execute as a final drawing on illustration board. How to transfer the pencil outline from the tracing paper to the illustration board? Here is one method that you might wish to try: having plotted the subject matter on a fairly good quality tracing paper, with auxiliary entourage blocked in and assuming the composition is satisfactory, I proceed by cutting off all peripheral work with a pair of scissors, leaving intact the plotted outline of the main part of the drawing. The portion of the tracing paper that contains the pencil outline is attached to the illustration board with a strip of drafting tape along the top edge of the tracing paper. One may now denote the main points and critical features with a pointed drafting instrument or glass pin by pushing it through the tracing paper, leaving a light impression on the surface of the illustration board below. Start with two marks, fold the tracing paper up, and with an appropriate straight edge connect the two points lightly with a pointed 2H pencil. Fold down the tracing paper again and continue. Complex outlines may thus be transferred to the illustration board in a few minutes. Afterward, the tracing paper is removed from the board being worked on and temporarily taped to the original sheet. With the entire composition for reference, you can readily commit the entourage to the illustration board. The advantage of this method is that one may do all the preliminary work on tracing paper and thus leave the delicate drawing surface of the illustration board free from plotting lines, smudges, and erasures, which are frequently part of preliminary outline and composition work. Presentation drawings on full-size sheets of illustration board at times embrace several perspectives of a building as they do plans, sections, and so forth. By doing preliminary outline work on tracing paper at the scale in which it is to be delineated, you can shift the various fragments around until you arrive at an aggregate satisfactory composition of the presentation. Examples of such drawings occur elsewhere in this book.

Preliminaries

A65

A delightful experience was in store when a client asked me to design a vacation house on a steep rocky site overlooking the ocean. The actual presentation drawing for the project is shown in illustration B38. The drawing presented here is based on the preliminary perspective drawing, which was plotted on tracing paper. Station point and elevation were chosen to express the configuration of the structure as clearly as possible and also to give the impression of rugged steepness, which is the outstanding feature of the site. Trees in abundance cover the area and so became part of the composition. All elements were drawn with a 2H pointed pencil. One more important decision was to be made, however—values. To this end, quick value studies are prepared, as shown in the next illustrations. Trees and the most obvious features of the site were drawn from photographs taken on site visits. Photographs like these are helpful in presentation work; they allow you to accurately portray the many elements that are to become part of the presentation drawing, and thus to add a sense of reality to your work.

A66

The value study shown here and
the one in the next illustration will
give you a clue as to how to
proceed. Normally, these studies
are not quite as elaborate and
detailed as this. They were quickly
roughed out on tracing paper, laid
over the plotted outline
perspective. It took approximately
ten minutes to draw them. Only a
soft pencil is used for this purpose;
with practice, you will be able to
lay down diverse tones without
difficulty. The light source here is
assumed to come from the left.
The shading of elements clearly
identifies this source. The sky is
dark, silhouetting the structure
and trees strongly against it. Now
let us look at another approach.

A67

The feeling has changed considerably. The light source, now from the right of the picture, casts interesting shadows. The light tone of the sky permits dark background trees to contrast sharply, as they do against the structure, which now becomes the center of interest by forming a silhouette in light tones against a darker surface. A few broad pencil strokes determine foreground and general configuration of the site to complete the preliminary work. This value study shows more promise than the one in illustration A66 and is chosen to form the basis for the pencil drawing in the next illustration. In many instances, rough pencil sketches such as these are sufficient to transmit ideas and objectives to a client. They are certainly explicit enough to serve as preliminary design studies, but they do not compare with a detailed drawing meticulously executed.

After accurately transposing the plotted perspective sketch from the tracing paper to the illustration board with a 2H pointed pencil lead, you are ready to begin. Keeping in mind the value study, which you should have nearby for reference, you might proceed with the darkest tones to the rear of the building. Allow some of the smaller pines in the background to stand out slightly by rendering them in a dark tone. Their forms will thus be made recognizable against the black background. All taller trees are left white at this stage and our efforts are directed toward the building, which receives various tones of gray put down with a 2H conically shaped pencil, each stroke roughly representing the width of one board. Note that depth of tone varies from one board to the next, as is the case in reality. Window areas are drawn in black pencil and shaded areas receive a "wash" with a conically shaped F lead pencil put down in broad strokes in the direction of falling light. Deeper tones on selected surfaces provide contrast and help to identify planes. A few figures provide scale. Elements in the left foreground are rendered quickly and decisively with broad strokes. In keeping with the direction of the light, tree trunks receive deeper tones on the left, in addition to the occasional diagonal dash of gray, which gives form to the round trunks.

A68

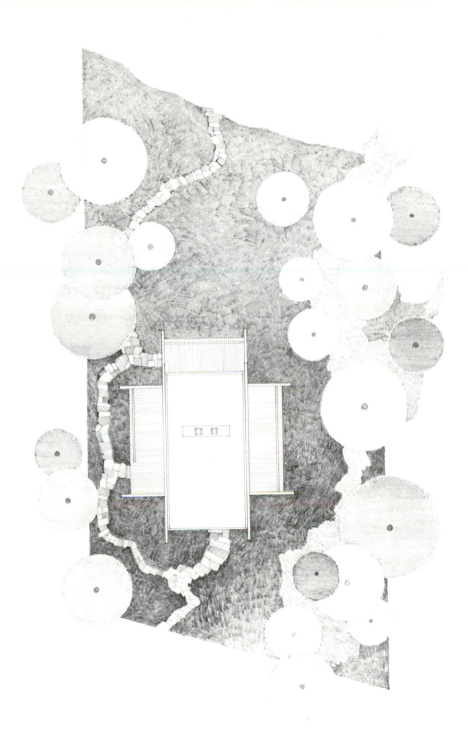

A69

In this example, the vacation house is shown in plan view with exactness, as though one were looking down on it from an elevated position. Although the site, trees, and stone path are sketched in accurately in terms of locating the natural elements, they are drawn freely, more in keeping with nature. Miscellaneous information concerning the site is omitted, not to confuse, but rather to concentrate on the main features. Depending on the circumstances, this approach is more appropriate at times. All the elements you wish to include on a site plan sketch of this kind are drawn in. The trees, of varying species, are represented by circles of differing diameters, to roughly identify their size. Keeping in mind how the stone path might be constructed, we sketch it in lightly. The shrubbery is indicated. With an F, broad, conically shaped pencil you can give property you are concerned with a textured tone of varying grays, achieved by changing both the direction of the pencil strokes and the intensity with which you press down on the drawing surface. In this way, you can carefully delineate property line, trees, the shrubbery, path, and, of course, the building. Refer to illustration A1 now for a review. Some of the circular patterns representing the trees are given a tone of gray by means of broad horizontal strokes. Shrubbery is indicated by more sketchy strokes. The key to this drawing is contrast with harmony. You will probably encounter many such situations for almost all buildings are surrounded by a land surface. That's why you should know how it might be represented. Now try it yourself.

A70

A quickly executed sketch of wood framed buildings under construction can be done with an F and 2B pencil, a small panel of illustration board, and a few minutes of time at the construction site. Although very little time was devoted to the sketch, it embodies the many principles discussed in this chapter.

Thus far, our main concern has been to represent the many elements that form the multitude of situations you will encounter. Graphite pencil, known to civilized people for ages and one of the most versatile tools, is used extensively to commit thoughts to paper. It has been the focus of this chapter. It is the basis of virtually all graphic art, whether it is the delineation of an abstract nude, the preliminary sketch to an oil painting depicting the Taj Mahal, or the portrait of a president. It is a grave mistake to think that you can forego this most important part of your work in an effort to progress more rapidly. Let us first learn how to draw with a pencil.

PART TWO

Pen and Ink and Colored Pencil on Tracing Paper and Illustration Board

You are now prepared for the work involved in the lessons that follow. If we assume that your studies have gone well, what you have learned up to this point will provide you with a sense of confidence in your work. Pencil work will still remain the principal drawing technique of the design process. However, ink alone, or in combination with colored crayon pencils, will give fine, natural effects, which lend themselves extraordinarily to architectural design and presentation work. We will therefore attempt this technique now, beginning with the study and application of simple textures, and progressing to color work, which will lead to complete presentation drawings of the type used for submission to clients or for publication.

Your success in this endeavor will depend greatly on the efforts you devote to practice. Do not skip sections of these lessons. Proceed as directed, for the lessons will ultimately permit you to be at ease with any problem you encounter. Your own style will inevitably emerge, but remember that the methods and procedures presented here are based on years of practice, not without frequent respite to pause and think about what was being achieved. In teaching this technique, I have found that students respond quickly when they are asked to prepare sound presentation drawings. Needless to say, drawing with a pen, particularly the type that can produce fine constant black lines, lends itself well to the detailed delineation of objects. One is able to produce an infinite variety of textures. The addition of color produces the kind of muted tones needed to add a sense of reality. The intensity of color in each case will depend on the circumstances. Buildings to be constructed in an area of virtually constant sunshine should express this setting when delineated prior to their construction. Conversely, to depict a concrete building in a northern wet climate in rose colors under a sky of cloudless blue is not only inaccurate but plainly dishonest. Buildings constructed of different materials and located in unlike environments will react differently to the weathering process. At this point you have the opportunity to test what you know about this subject and express it in your drawing.

You will have to know a great deal about the way buildings are constructed if your drawing is to be credible. Throughout history, the appearance of structures and their style of ornament

Introduction

have been determined by the technical ability to construct them, as well as by the tools employed to shape the building materials available. The form of contemporary architecture is no different. The science of mechanics influences the forms of buildings we design and thus a basic knowledge of this subject is clearly an asset. Let us now consider the equipment you will require to work on the lessons of this chapter. An art or architectural supply store will probably have the materials you need.

First, you will need some good quality drawing pens. Rapidograph technical fountain pens are my favorite. For flexibility, I suggest three point thicknesses—size 3X0, 00, and 2. These precision manufactured drawing devices are filled with india ink of appropriate quality and are most suitable for freehand drawing, or may be used in combination with straight edges. The pens are color coded so unnecessary guessing is avoided as you work on a drawing since each color represents a different point size. Additional accessories are available, the details of which can be fully explained to you by sales staff in a graphics material store.

For the drawing surface, I use Hi-Art no. 62. The texture of the surface of this illustration board is a good compromise—it accepts ink well and yet possesses sufficient abrasive characteristics to allow an effective application of colored pencils. For pure ink drawings, you may use illustration board with a smoother surface. Many types and qualities are available. As you are aware, ink can be difficult to erase and errors are sometimes unavoidable. Therefore, you should have on hand a small jar of white tempera paint and a fine brush so you can paint out ink work that you would rather not see on your drawing. The color of the white tempera paint matches the color of most illustration board surfaces fairly well so that corrections will remain almost unnoticed.

High quality, thick, colored pencils complete the list of materials required. Colored pencils are available in assorted sets, but it is probably best to buy them individually in order to select the most appropriate ones for your work. If you have on hand more than you require, you will merely become confused and your work more difficult. Keep in mind that any two or more colors may be combined to form an intermediate shade. Thus you have virtually unlimited scope in the range from potent primary colors to the subtle hues of pastels. I regularly employ nine colors, which give me all the versatility I require whether I am studying color schemes for proposed buildings or executing complex presentation drawings: red, orange, light blue, dark blue, light brown, dark brown, ochre, olive green, and yellow. Ultimately you will delete some and add some for you will establish your own way of working. Moreover, the types of illustrations you undertake will by necessity determine the materials you employ. As you are about to start your first exercises in ink, remember that the ink work must be fairly well completed before you apply colored pencils; the desirable depths in a drawing should be fully established, for the success of all succeeding color work is dependent on it. The exercises recommended in the following lessons are invaluable and in fact are the basis for color work.

B1

These eight panels depicting different tones with varying degrees of intensities drawn with ink pens probably sum up the range of textures you can expect in the presentation work discussed here. You may invent your own, but to get you started, practice these until you are able to put them down on illustration board with ease. Then, you might like to add to them pen work that is more to your liking and possibly more suited to the work you do. The exercise panels presented here were produced as follows: Rapid, circular motions with a 00 pen obtained the results in (a). A finer point size applied similarly but with less pressure yielded (b). Exercise (c) consists of short, multidirectional lines, while (d) is produced by the method in (a), except that the circles are smaller, reveal less white, and thus produce a darker tone. Carefully applied lines with a fine point thickness pen resulted in the texture in (e). In panel (f), fine lines, rapidly executed across each other produced this texture. In (g), diagonal lines applied freehand cross each other in a maze. The final panel (h) consists of fine vertical lines put down freehand. Anyone able to hold a pen should be able to draw these. The creditability of an architectural drawing will depend on the knowledge of the texture of the materials one wishes to depict and how they are assembled. The following drawings exemplify this point.

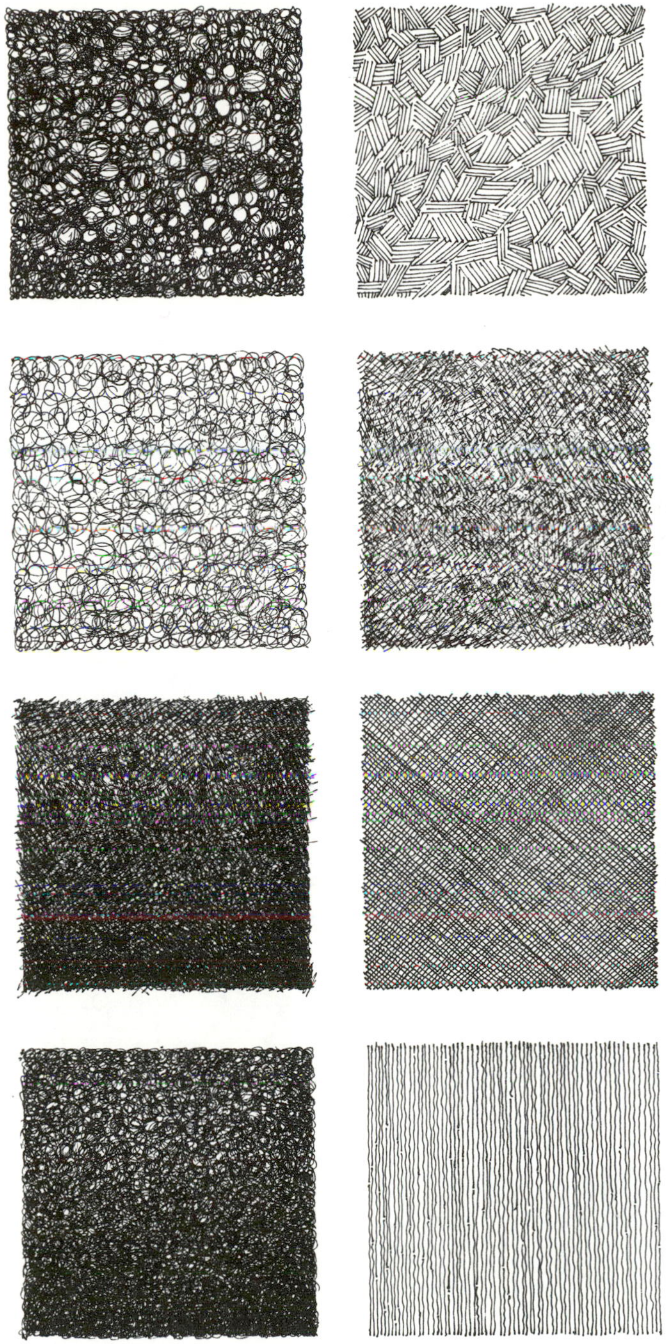

(a)

(b)

(c)

(d)

(e)

(f)

(g)

(h)

B2

The outline of the brick wall and steel gate here are drawn with drafting instruments, and then the shrubbery is blocked in. All features are drawn freehand with a pen. To the left, color work was omitted to allow for an examination of the drawing prior to the application of crayon, which was begun by applying a tone of blue to the entire surface prior to the application of additional colors. The brickwork consists of varying hues of red and orange, permitting occasional bricks to appear in deeper tones. The gate is simply depicted in tones of blue, the uprights left white for contrast against the darker foliage beyond. The concrete coping at the top of the wall is depicted with short vertical strokes with a pointed 2H lead. Shrubbery is indicated by a few dashes with green crayon. Diagonal strokes with a 2H lead pencil establish the direction of light and complete the drawing. Study all features carefully with a view to understanding why they are presented in this way. Now you will wish to work on your own drawing—good luck in your first encounter with drawing in this context.

B3

*The approach in depicting this stone wall is similar to that used in
the previous illustration, although additional colors were used to give
greater variety of hues to the individual stones. Experiment until you
arrive at color combinations that appear real, are visually interesting,
and merge well into the total drawing.*

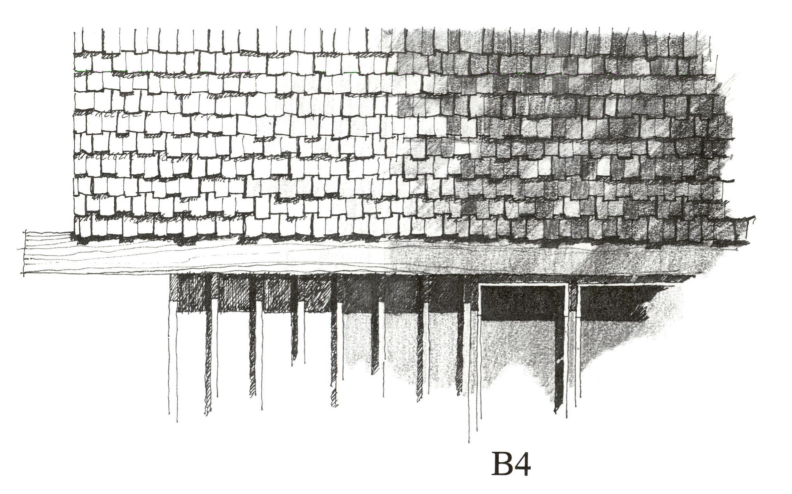

B4

Shakes, uneven, gray and weathered, cover the roof structure of a board and batten enclosed building. Colors employed are few and muted by the superimposition of graphite pencil work. Contrast is achieved through the dark values applied in ink and light surfaces such as the window frames occurring against these. Kept white, they become sharply delineated. Start this exercise by putting the general configurations of all elements on the illustration board with pencil and drafting instruments. Follow with ink work, remembering that the desired contrast is achieved by making surfaces in shade quite dark. Note the uneven shadows cast by the shakes, which give them a realistic appearance. Muted tones of light blue and ochre were applied gently over some of the surfaces and a stronger tone of blue in glazed areas completed this study.

B5

This outdoor sketch executed on a sketching trip embraces many of the principles discussed thus far. Take an hour, weather permitting, and do one of these on the spot. Rough out trunk and branch formations with a pencil. Apply ink work, with a view to creating the essential contrast. Apply color from the range of colored pencils recommended in this chapter and produce a small outdoor study of a grouping of leafless branches.

B6

A grove of alders, one fallen to the saw, was the basis of this sketch completed in thirty minutes. Muted tones and high contrast contributed to the visual interest of this simple subject.

B7

A grouping of young and mature evergreens reaching upward from dense undergrowth are delineated with ink pen over a pencil outline done beforehand. Composition and contrast are the main contributing features. The ink work complete, color was applied over inked surfaces in a few minutes. The distant hills were done in a light blue, adding interest and depth to this sketch. A few foreground forms reminiscent of flowering plants were indicated with intense colors. Delineating tree forms convincingly demands discipline and a careful study of these forms.

B8

The trees, their form, and the manner of their portrayal is self-explanatory. Dark, shaded foliage is the key to this drawing. Branches in lighter tones occurring against a dark background (and vice versa) lend realism. The palette is minimal: dark blue, green, and ochre.

B9

This drawing is based on an old black-and-white photograph. The *general structure of the trees was blocked in, and fence posts and flowering shrubs indicated. Ink work established depth and the required contrast. Flowers, their scale accentuated for interest, occur against a dark background. The sketch is visually pulled together by fine strokes, freely applied, which allow all the elements to merge. The colors for the foliage of the tree are dark blue and ochre; the trunk, brown and red, applied lightly. A gentle application of light blue in appropriate areas, strong colors in varying intensities for flowers, and a few dashes with green crayon complete this study.*

B10

Your opportunity to practice fine pen work is everywhere. To compose a sketch from the most simple subjects is an interesting challenge. You may think that many features are ordinary and surfaces flat and uninteresting. But are they? Look again. Take a brick, for example. It is possible to bring out features that are characteristic of the material and its manufacture. Introduce shade and shadow for interest and contrast. A 3X0 pen was used to complete all the ink work in this sketch after a pencil outline had been made. Dark blue, applied in varying intensities, comprised the next step. The brick received hues of red, and graphite pencil was used to tone them down. Studies like these help you to improve your powers of observation, and they have traditionally been the basis of training in the fine arts. If you do many of them, you will benefit immensely.

B11

Putting figures into an architectural presentation drawing is not only a necessity at times but also a simple matter, as you will discover by using the accompanying sketch as a basis. With a 3X0 pen, draw the figures directly on illustration board. Textures, freely applied to clothing, give the required variety. Contrast is achieved by allowing dark surfaces to occur against lighter areas and light or white highlights to appear in an area of dark tones. With the quickly applied pen work completed, color, in a multitude of tones and intensities, was superimposed where appropriate. Areas appearing too intense were simply muted by a few dashes with a graphite pencil. If you wish to study some of the many poses people assume, equip yourself with a camera to which you can attach a telephoto lens. Now go to a public area, street, or park, and photograph some of the postures you find interesting. Let the prints be the basis for a few sketches depicting human figures. Then commit them to your portfolio. You will need them at the most unexpected moments!

B12

You are looking at a pencil outline
of a side elevation of a Cobra
Hardtop. The basis for the drawing
of this beautiful antique sports car
was a photograph that I had taken
years ago. It seemed a good
subject matter for acquiring the
facility to draw automobiles in
color. Using a straight edge and
compass, you will be able to block
in the general form precisely in
pencil, and then can move on to
the ink work in confidence.

B13

Carefully study the textures produced here by a 3X0 pen. All the surfaces appearing black at first glance are actually not—minute portions of the white surface are permitted to show, and thus give a realistic appearance of the various textures, particularly the tires, spoked wheels, and the hard top. The deep shadow beneath the car joins it with the road surface on which it rests.

B14

A mixture of dark and light blue, applied strongly and decisively with colored pencils, was put down on the painted areas of the body. A hint of blue was put on the windshield, side vents, areas of the wheels, and tires in shade. Lights, reflectors, and brake drums (visible through the spokes) received a hint of orange. Areas considered too bright were muted with a graphite pencil. The luster on the body was highlighted with white tempera applied with a brush. And thus we have an interpretation of a timeless automobile.

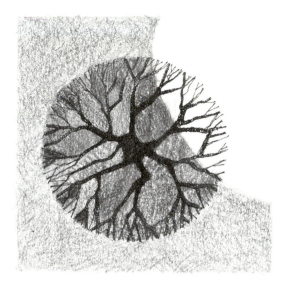

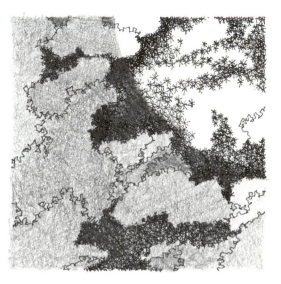

B15

B16

B17

The sketches shown here illustrate many of the symbols I employ in the preparation of presentation drawings. A portion of each has been left incomplete to indicate the ink work that preceded the application of color and graphite. Try to represent these symbols; when you have succeeded, invent some of your own to use in your work. Experimentation will guide you to your own ways of expressing these indispensable elements in architectural presentation work.

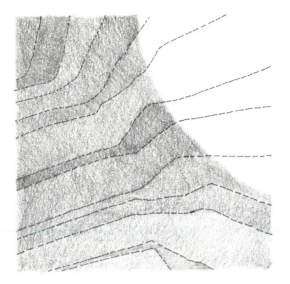

B18

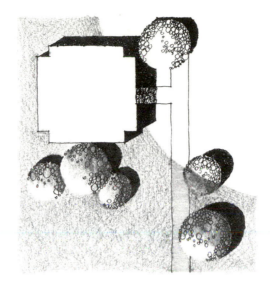

B19

B20

B21

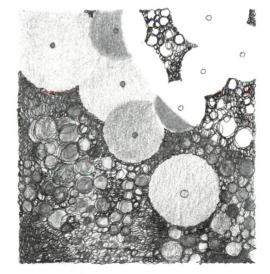

B22

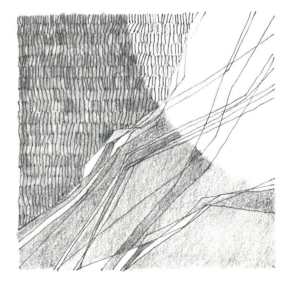

B23

B24

This portion of a metal curtain wall facade, the type of building enclosure common in all regions of North America, is presented here in three stages of completion. One needs to know something about the actual details of the metal frames and panels before drawing them. The system depicted here consists of continuous vertical mullions of anodized aluminum. Window sills and wall panels of the same material are represented somewhat darker to distinguish the different elements. The freehand pen work, based on a pencil outline, was followed by a tone of blue, lightly and evenly applied to the panels. Cast shadows are inked in. The final step included an application of ochre to all metal parts, resulting in a greenish tinge on the panels. The sills and vertical mullions are toned down with graphite lead. Glazing is represented with light blue crayon muted with graphite. Reflective metal and glass facades mirror neighboring structures and objects, as they do the sky. In order to represent a proposed building realistically, you may need a photograph of these in order to show them accurately. In this drawing the reflected buildings are indicated by deeper tones accomplished by the application of additional pen work, dark blue crayon, and lead pencil.

B25

An elevation of a house discussed in Part One is shown here in four stages of completion. The outline of the structure is drawn with pencil and drafting instruments. The entourage is blocked in. Pen work was completed as is indicated for the second stage. Prior to actual color work to define individual elements, the entire drawing surface, with occasional exceptions for highlight, received a light and even application of dark blue, enriching the final drawing with a fine atmospheric effect. Automobiles and human figures lend scale to the drawing. All textures have their basis in illustration B1. Perhaps you should examine them once more before beginning presentation work.

B26

This uninteresting photograph did not really form the background to the sketch shown in illustration B27. It was taken afterwards to demonstrate a point. Please read on.

B27

This quickly drawn sketch of floating sheds and boat houses was done on the spot on a late autumn afternoon when I came upon this scene by chance. It gives a record of the elements present, which have been shifted around for compositional purposes. The photograph in illustration B26 was unable to do that. In particular, it lacks detail in the dimness of the shaded areas of the buildings, which are left obscure.

B28

Distant snow-capped mountains are seen from the bank of a small creek. An example of a quickly executed rendition of an outdoor scene.

B29

Muted tones of crayon over freely sketched ink work is used to represent boat houses drawn from memory. It's a scene I was lured to for its nostalgic quality. It is a good example of a freehand sketch, the kind one should be able to do readily for enjoyment and to practice one's hand, as well as to quickly record a setting if the need arises.

B30

This drawing was also done freehand, but in order to express the sharp features of this architectural project realistically, greater care was exercised in its execution. The 3X0 pen work throughout gives the drawing a delicate feeling. Only a few colors were employed, mostly blues and greens, which were muted by the liberal use of graphite in nearly all parts of the drawing.

B31

This is a freehand pencil sketch on tracing paper rapidly drawn as part of preliminary design studies for a prefabrication system I developed a few years ago. The time it took to produce this sketch was probably no more than thirty minutes, yet it contains all the elements needed for study. Again, note that contrast plays a vital role in allowing individual elements to be identified readily.

B32

The small house roughly sketched in the previous illustration is here carefully delineated in ink and colored pencils. To indicate the procedure employed in the preparation, I have left portions of the drawing only partly completed. The pencil outline shown in the upper left, which includes all entourage, preceded delicate ink work done freehand with a 3X0 pen. Tones of blue in varying intensities were put over most areas of the drawing. This was followed by color work, which completed the project. Deep, darkly drawn shadows on glass and siding and the darkly rendered sky are important areas that give the required contrast and define architectural and natural features.

B33

The handsome high rise concrete structure shown in this photograph is the center of our attention in this lesson. The elevated station point from which the photographer took the picture best revealed the features of the building after it was built. Our problem is to choose a station point in relation to the building before it has been erected. Thus, your first step is to choose that point so that you can proceed to plot a perspective from sketch plans or working drawings. If we are satisfied that an aerial view of the project is the best choice, we can then plot the proposed building accurately on tracing paper. Nearby buildings and background are blocked in, usually from photographs taken for this purpose. We are now ready to transfer the pencil outline work to the illustration board. The next step is to establish desirable values, and to that end the following two sketches were prepared.

B34

B35

In order to best define the configuration of the building, the direction of light first had to be established. Value studies quickly done served this purpose. Light from the right, as in illustration B34, shows off the elegance of the narrow facade and the interesting base of the building, but the side of the building penetrated by windows appears gloomy. Illustration B35 with the light source on the left allows for greater contrast on the facade pierced by the windows. It also more clearly defines the shape of the buildings. We will therefore select it as the basis for the drawing in the next illustration.

B36

The step-by-step procedure employed in preparing a drawing of this kind is illustrated by showing it in four stages of development. An accurate pencil outline is followed by freehand ink work with a 3X0 pen. Concrete surfaces in shade received a "tone" of multiple horizontal lines to concur with the actual texture of board-formed concrete. Nearby buildings and background were drawn with less attention to detail. The next step included additional ink work in areas where this produces desirable contrast. A tone of blue was applied to all surfaces except those to be highlighted in the final phase. Colored pencils were employed to prepare for the finish: ochre was used for the buildings' surfaces reflected from a brilliant sky of the same color; and dashes of green and brown were used for miscellaneous trees and background, the surface of the water, the roofs of adjoining buildings, and the distant skyline. The mood for the final step was set: the liberal application of graphite with an F lead to bring required definition to particular surfaces and to bring harmony to the multitude of elements of which the drawing is comprised. The result is a moody rendition of a fine building. Now study this step-by-step description once more, relate it to the illustrations, and with confidence proceed to draw a building of your choice by employing a similar procedure.

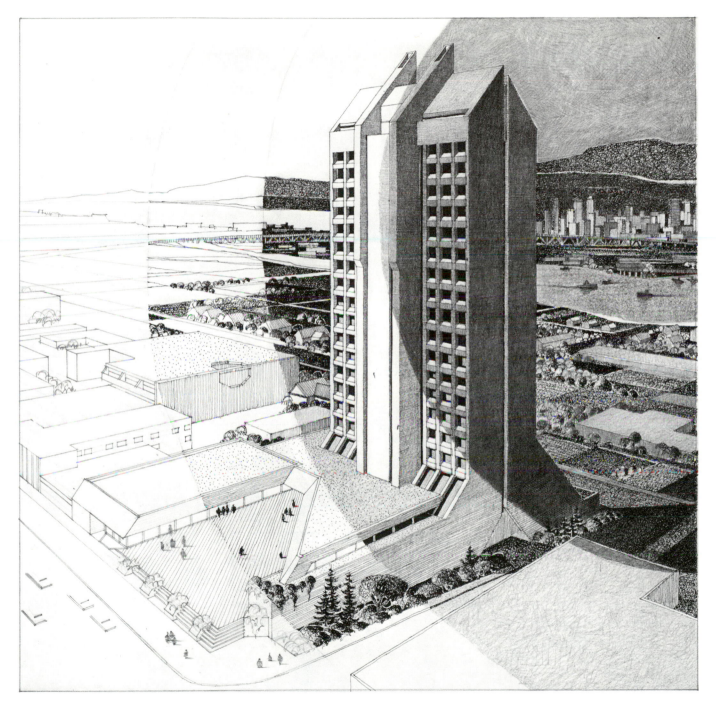

B37

Not all drawings produced during the design process are neat renditions of the future projects they are to represent. On the contrary, many such sketches merely show the essentials, giving the designer an opportunity to study site relationships, proportions, color, and any other applicable considerations. These sketches are a basic part of the process of arriving at satisfactory solutions and usually precede final presentation drawings. One such sketch study of a house drawn freehand to scale on tracing paper is included here. Become familiar with this part of design work and practice your hand by doing sketch studies like these at every opportunity; awkwardness will soon vanish and the joy of drawing will emerge as your ability improves.

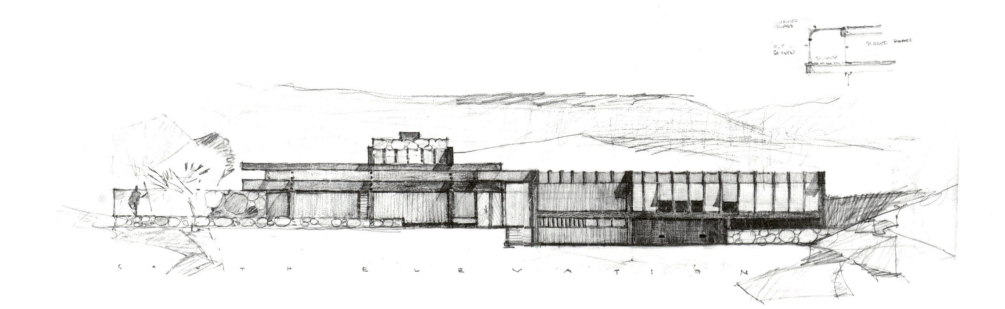

Illustrations B38 through B48 are presentation drawings produced as part of my architectural practice. The original size in most cases is equal to a full sheet of illustration board. The information in these drawings was largely dictated by the circumstances under which they were prepared, but they all served as a means of communicating to clients the appearance and character of the proposed projects. Drawn freely yet with considerable attention to detail, they are the direct result of the design process; that is to say, the proposed general configuration and the structure of the proposed projects are finalized at this stage. Critical aspects are featured so as to bring them into focus. Site characteristics, which are based on photographs, are accurately represented to lend realism. Virtually all graphic elements included here have been discussed in this chapter. Thus layout, or composition of the sheet, remains the critical issue. As this is a personal matter, the student should embark on an undertaking of this nature by experimenting until satisfactory results have been achieved. Since the possibilities are limitless, the subject remains fresh, each project posing its own unique challenges.

Presentation Drawings

B38

Opposite: Full drawing for summer house.

Page 104: View of house from south.

Page 105: Upper floor plan.

Page 106: Lower floor plan.

Page 107: Longitudinal section.

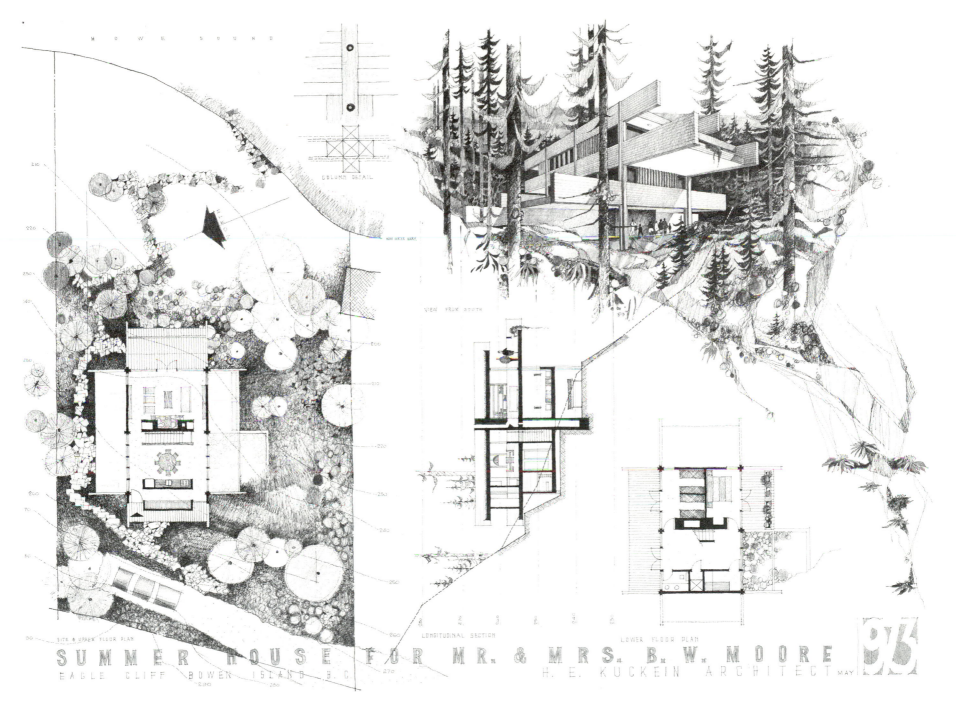

HOWE SOUND

COLUMN DETAIL

VIEW FROM SOUTH

SITE & UPPER FLOOR PLAN

LONGITUDINAL SECTION

LOWER FLOOR PLAN

SUMMER HOUSE FOR MR. & MRS. B. W. MOORE 93
EAGLE CLIFF BOWEN ISLAND B.C. H. E. KUCKEIN ARCHITECT MAY

104   PRESENTATION DRAWING (DETAIL)

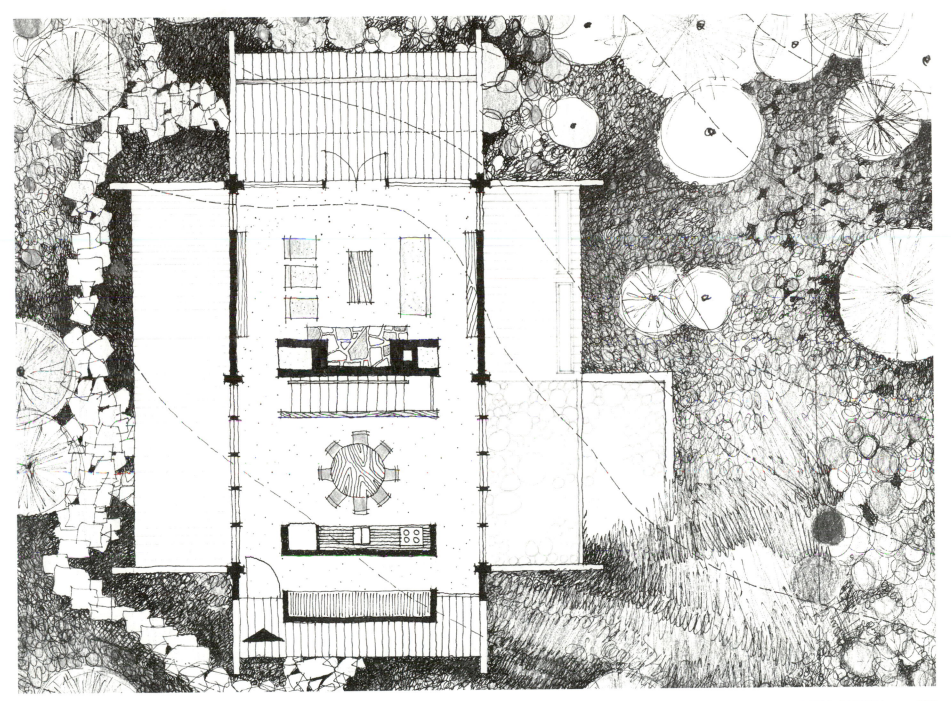

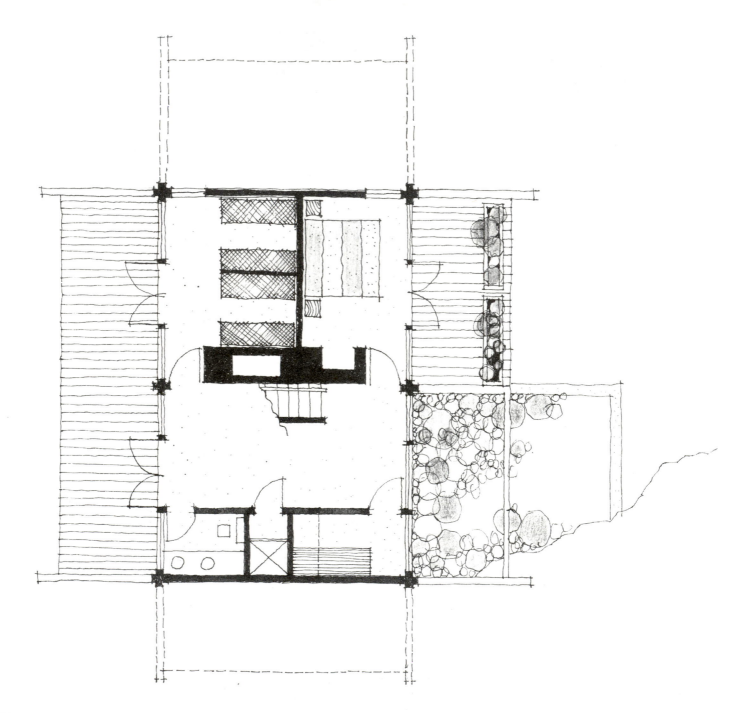

106   PRESENTATION DRAWING (DETAIL)

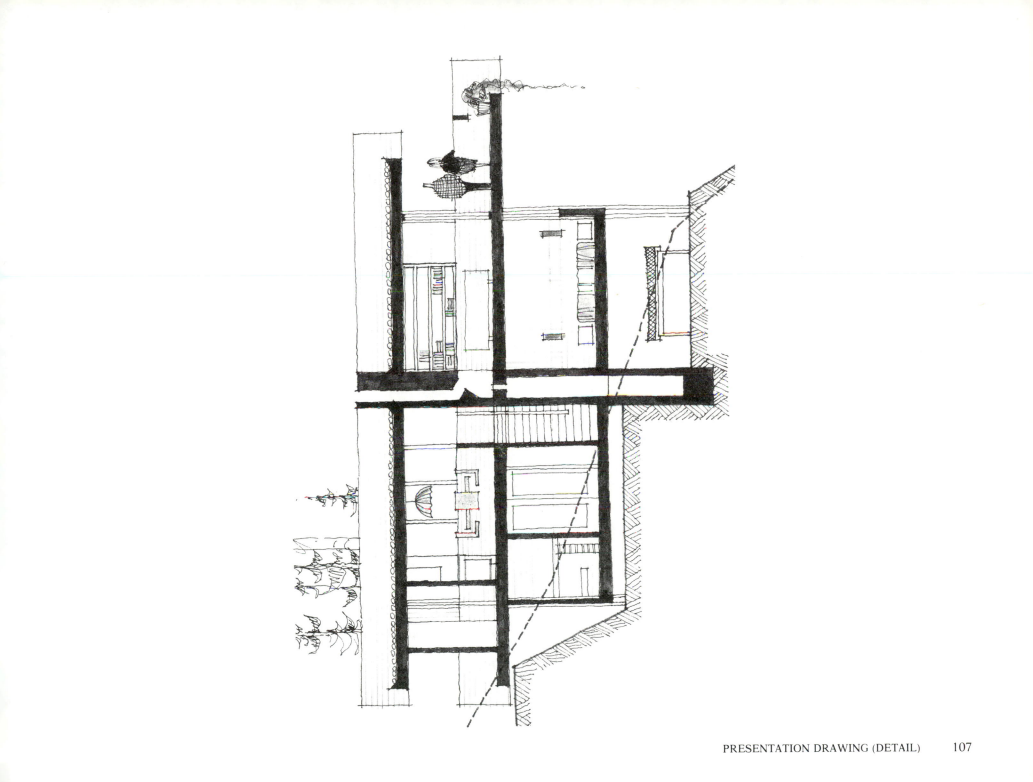

B39

Opposite: Full presentation drawing for a Berm House.

Page 110: Floor plan.

Page 111: View of house from southwest.

Page 112: View of kitchen-dining room.

Page 113: (Top) Sketch of north elevation; (bottom) west elevation.

ALTERNATIVE

WEST ELEVATION

NORTH ELEVATION

VIEW OF HOUSE FROM SOUTH-WEST

VIEW OF KITCHEN-DINING ROOM

NORTH

FLOOR PLAN & SITE DEVELOPMENT

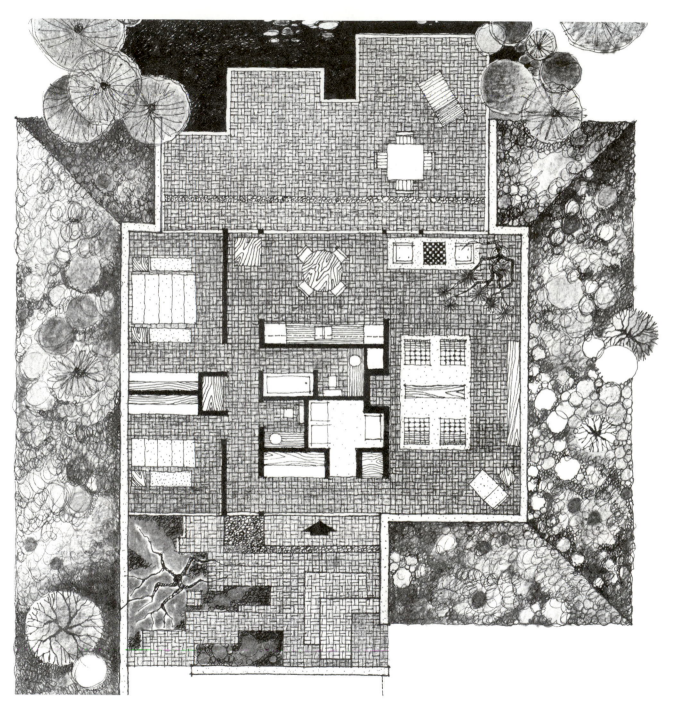

110   PRESENTATION DRAWING (DETAIL)

OF HOUSE FROM SOUTH-WEST

VIEW OF KITCHEN-DINING ROOM

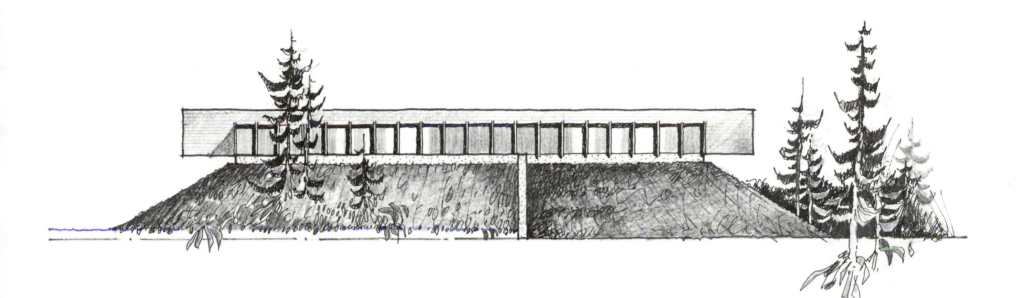

B40

Opposite: Full presentation drawing for a house and boutique.

Page 116: Main floor plan.

Page 117: View from southeast.

Page 118: Main entrance.

Page 119: Cross section.

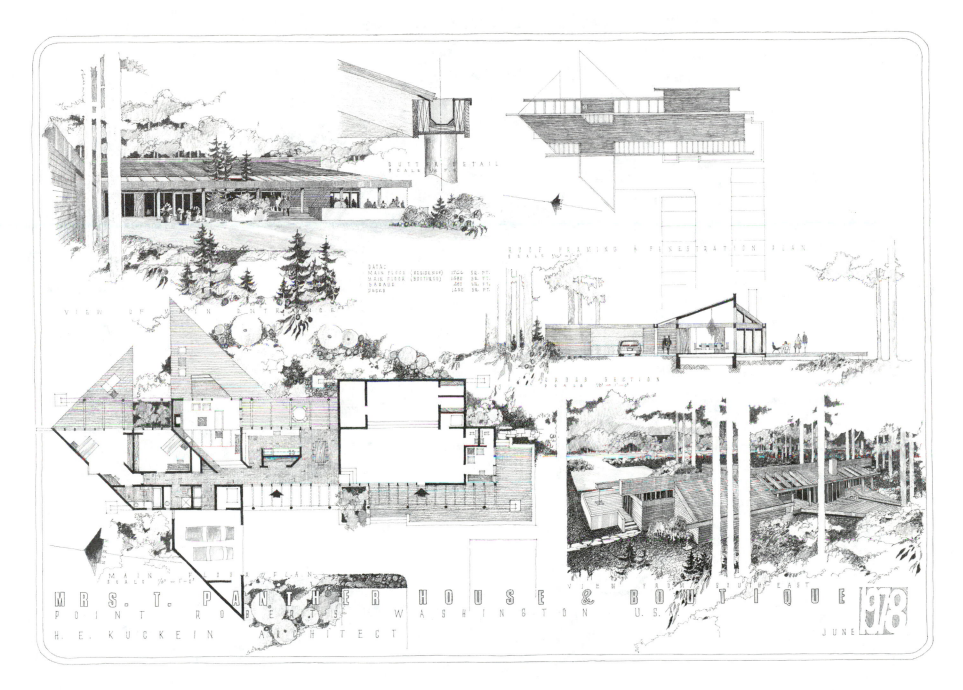

DATA:
MAIN FLOOR (RESIDENCE) 1700 SQ. FT.
MAIN FLOOR (BOUTIQUE)   1440 SQ. FT.
GARAGE   440 SQ. FT.
DECKS   1450 SQ. FT.

MRS. T. PANTHER HOUSE & BOUTIQUE
POINT ROBERTS WASHINGTON U.S.A.
H. E. KUCKEIN ARCHITECT

JUNE 1978

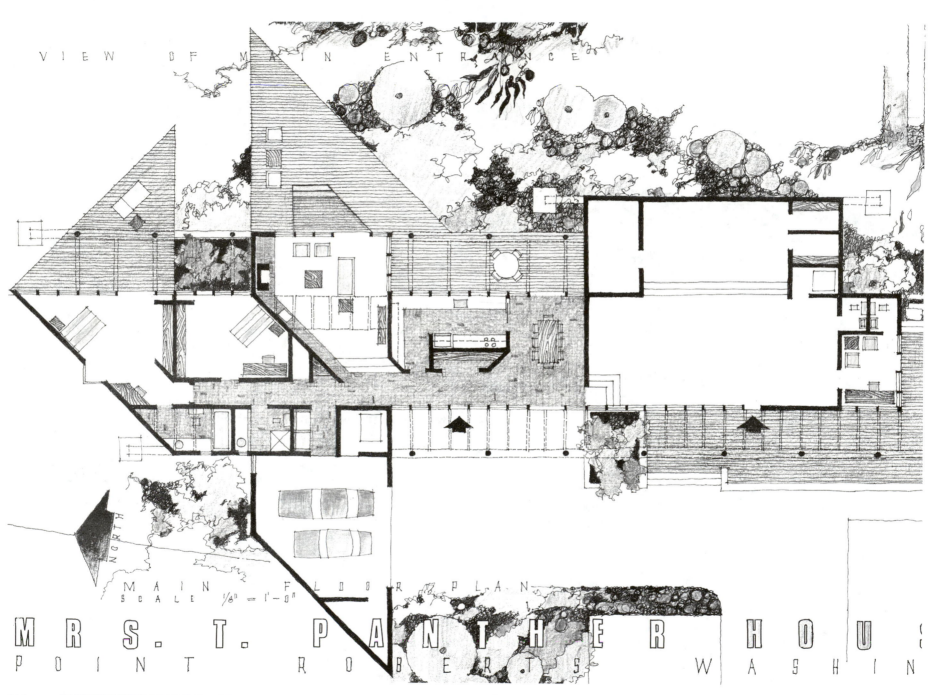

VIEW OF MAIN ENTRANCE

NORTH

MAIN FLOOR PLAN
SCALE 1/8" = 1'-0"

MRS. T. PANTHER HOUS
POINT ROBERTS WASHIN

VIEW FROM SOUTH-EAST

& BOUTIQUE 1978

ON U.S.A. JUNE

GUTTER DET
SCALE 1/8 F.S

DATA:
MAIN FLOOR (RESIDENCE)   1766 S
MAIN FLOOR (BOUTIQUE)   1480 S
GARAGE   480 S
DECKS   1450 S

OF MAIN ENTRANCE

E 1/16" = 1'-0"

C R O S S   S E C T I O N
S C A L E   1/8" = 1'-0"

B41

Opposite: Full presentation drawing for a country house.

Page 122: Upper floor plan.

Page 123: View of south facade.

Page 124: South elevation.

Page 125: (Left) Cross section; (right) site plan.

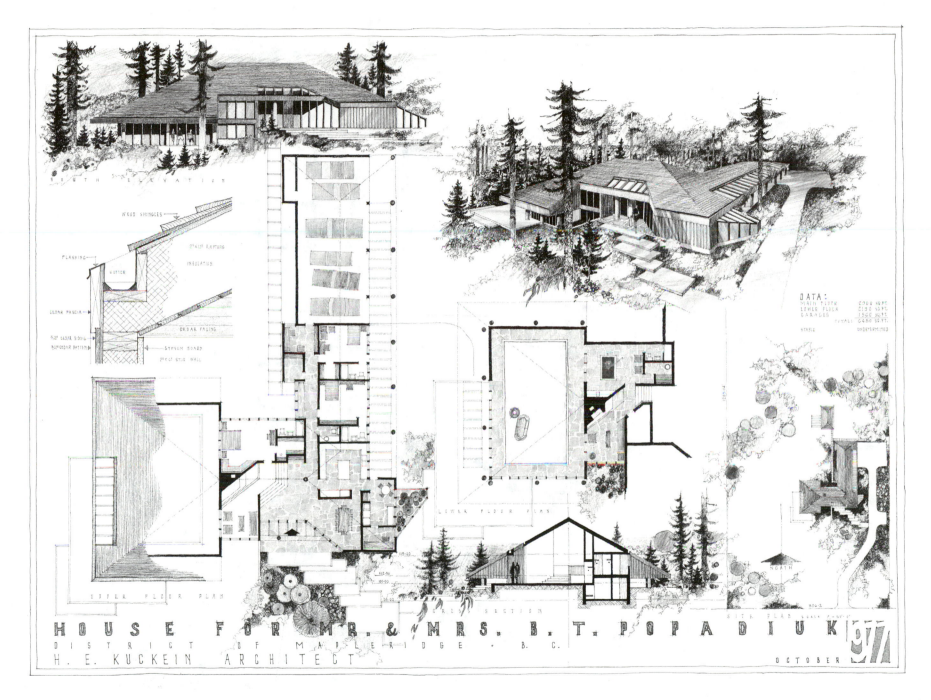

HOUSE FOR MR. & MRS. B. T. POPADIUK
DISTRICT OF MAPLE RIDGE · B. C.
H. E. KUCKEIN ARCHITECT

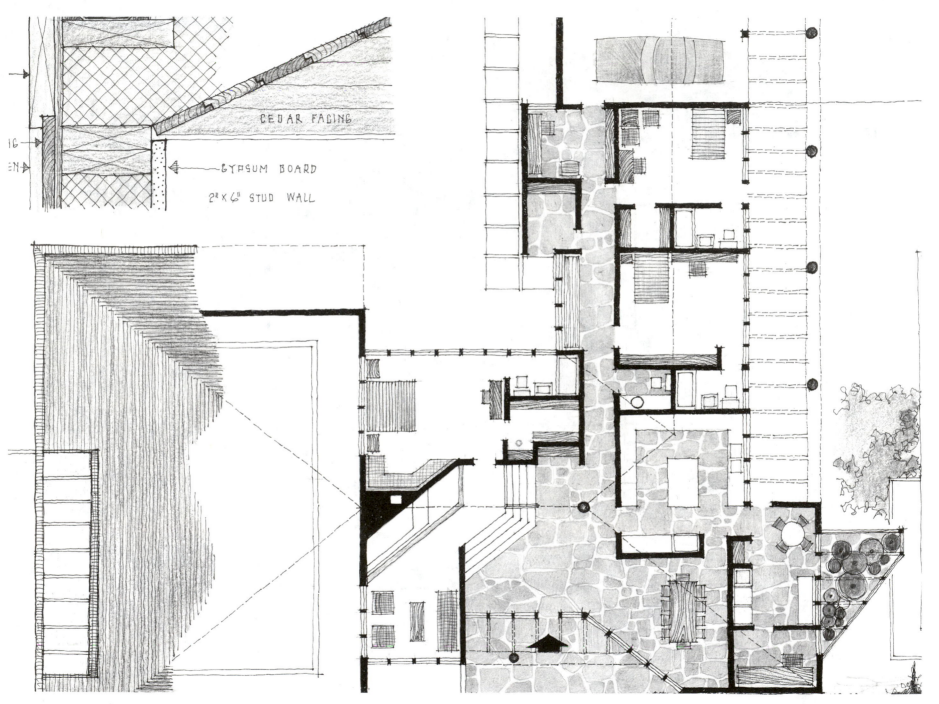

CEDAR FACING

GYPSUM BOARD

2" X 6" STUD WALL

E L E V A T I O N

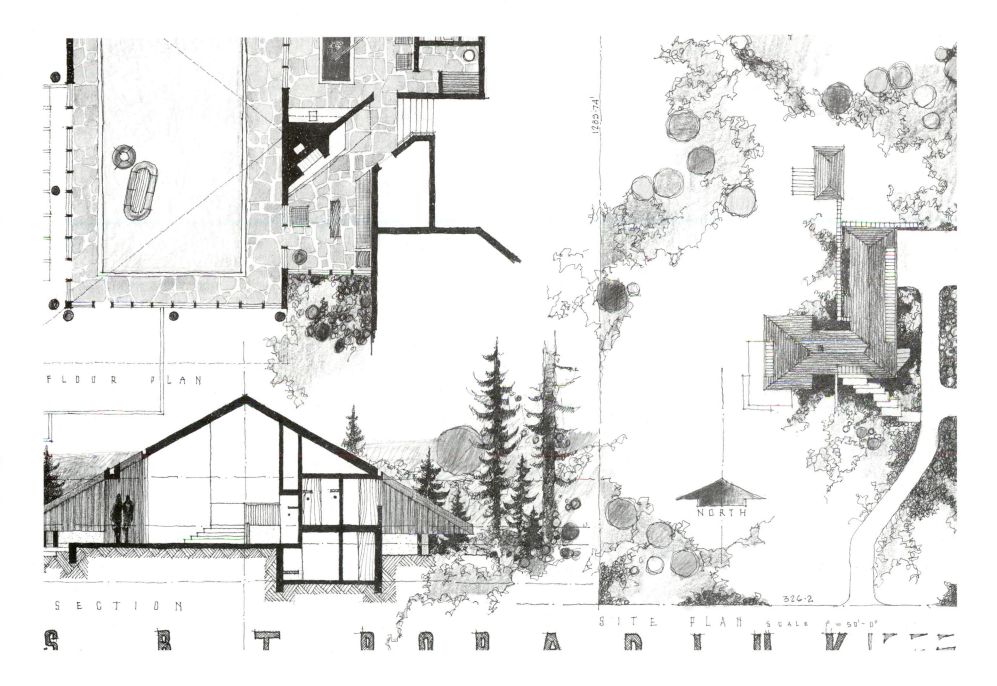

FLOOR PLAN

SECTION

SITE PLAN SCALE 1" = 50'-0"

NORTH

B42

Opposite: Proposal drawing for a house near the ocean.

Page 128: Main floor plan.

Page 129: House showing swimming pool.

Page 130: Upper portion of site plan.

Page 131: Lower portion of site plan.

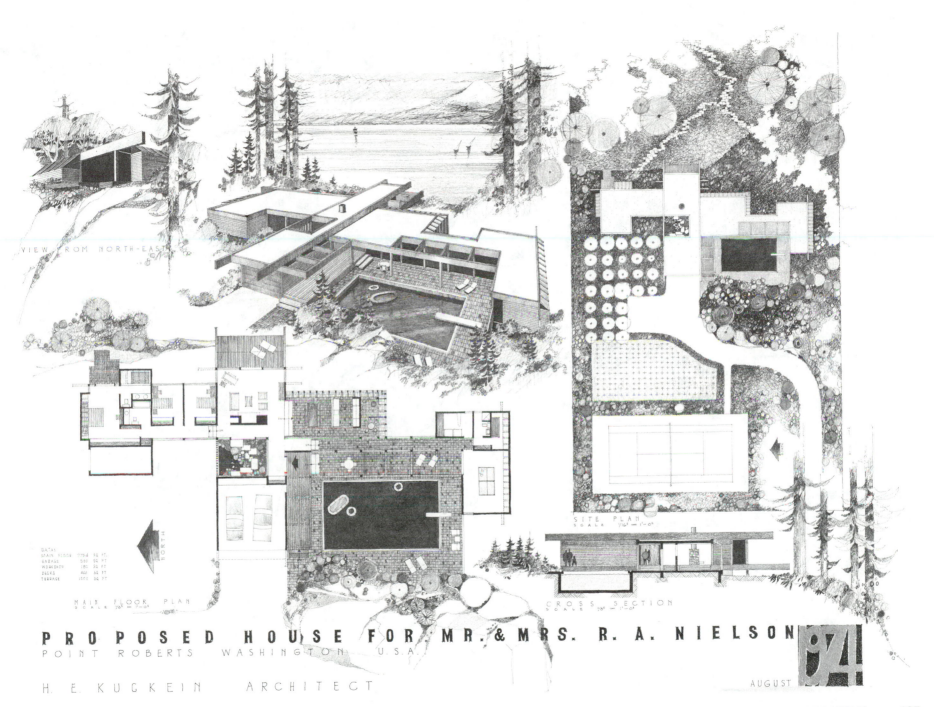

VIEW FROM NORTH-EAST

SITE PLAN
SCALE 1/16" = 1'-0"

MAIN FLOOR PLAN
SCALE 1/8" = 1'-0"

CROSS SECTION
SCALE 1/8" = 1'-0"

NORTH

DATA:
MAIN FLOOR 2784 SQ FT.
GARAGE   500 SQ FT
WORKSHOP   180 SQ FT
DECKS   400 SQ FT
TERRACE   1500 SQ FT

PROPOSED HOUSE FOR MR. & MRS. R. A. NIELSON

POINT ROBERTS WASHINGTON U.S.A.

H. E. KUCKEIN ARCHITECT

AUGUST '74

2754 SQ FT.
500 SQ FT
180 SQ FT
460 SQ FT
1000 SQ FT

MAIN FLOOR PLAN
SCALE 1/8" = 1'–0"

PROPOSED HOUSE FOR MR. &

NORTH

PRESENTATION DRAWING (DETAIL)

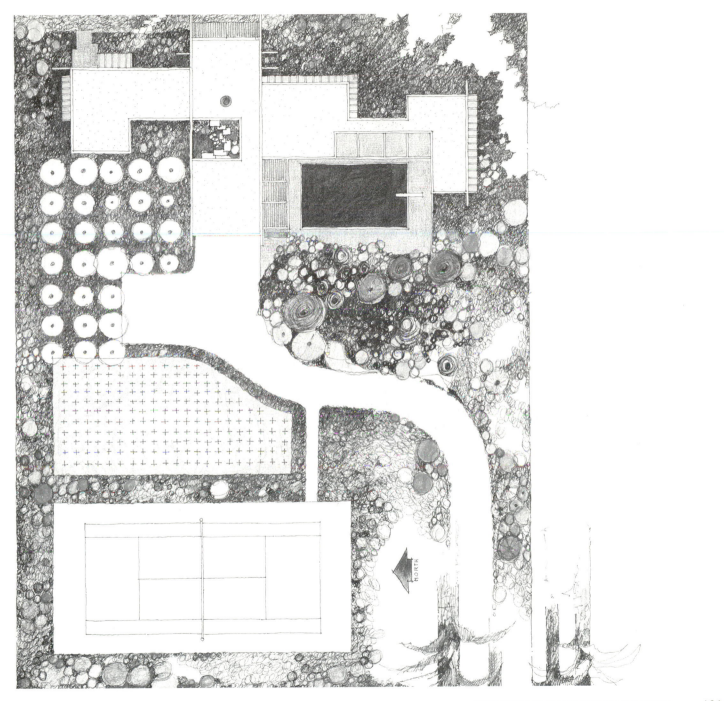

B43

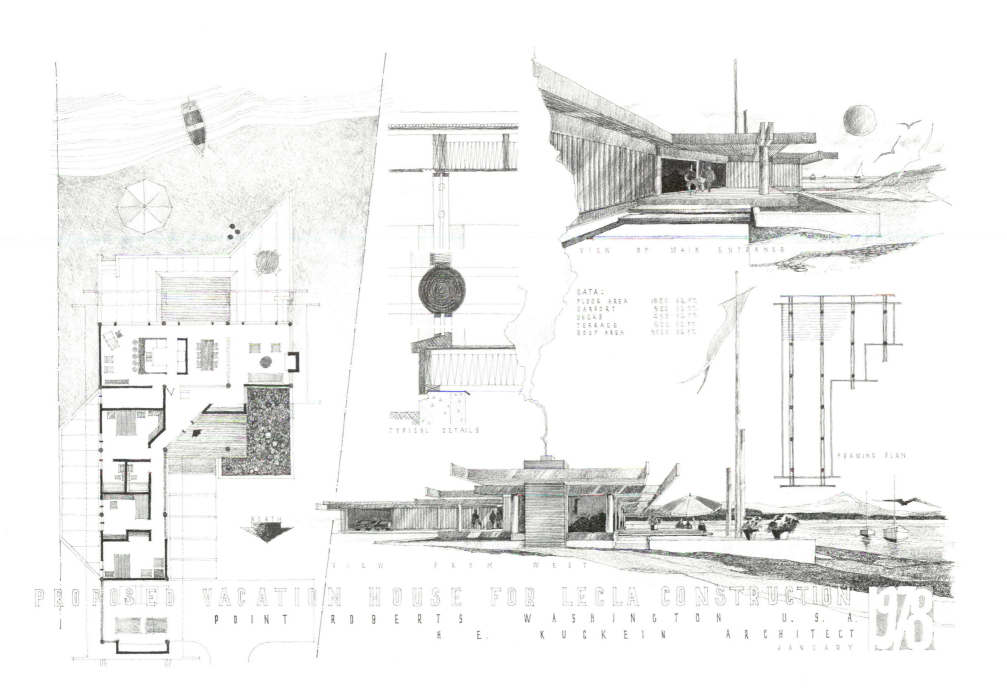

DATA:
FLOOR AREA   1820 SQ.FT.
CARPORT   320 SQ.FT.
DECKS   450 SQ.FT.
TERRACE   620 SQ.FT.
ROOF AREA   3000 SQ.FT.

VIEW OF MAIN ENTRANCE

TYPICAL DETAILS

FRAMING PLAN

NORTH

VIEW FROM WEST

PROPOSED VACATION HOUSE FOR LECLA CONSTRUCTION
POINT ROBERTS WASHINGTON U.S.A.
H. E. KUCKEIN ARCHITECT
JANUARY
1978

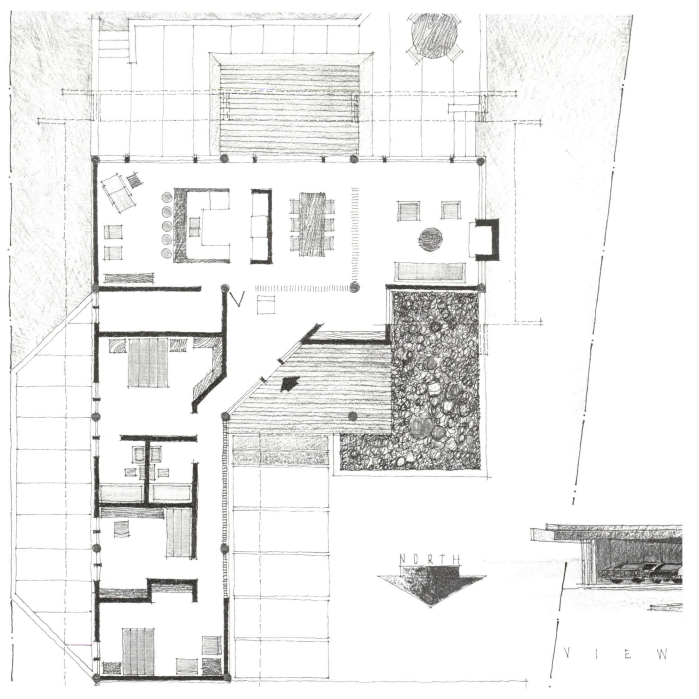

NORTH

VIEW

VIEW OF MAIN ENTRANCE

V I E W   F R O M   W E S T

PRESENTATION DRAWING (DETAIL)

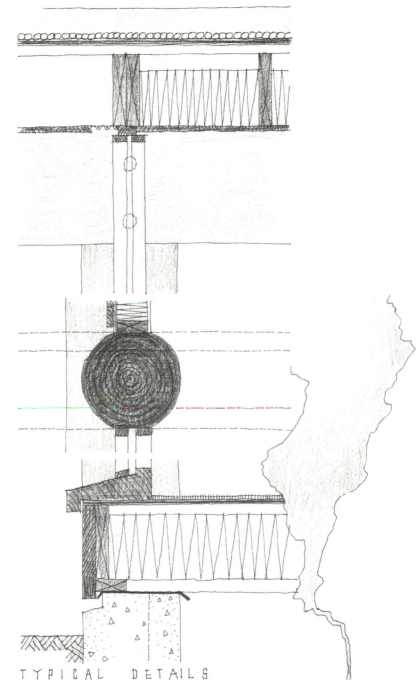

TYPICAL DETAILS

B44

VACATION HOUSE FOR DR. & MRS. J. CRAIB

POINT ROBERTS WASHINGTON U.S.A.

H. E. KUCKEIN ARCHITECT

FEBRUARY

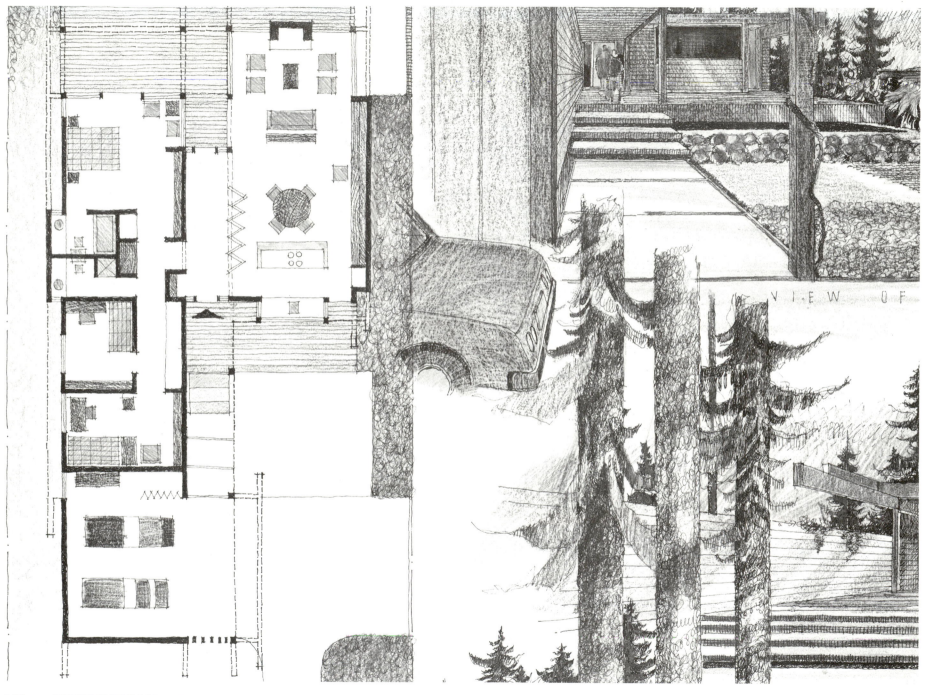

VIEW OF

142   PRESENTATION DRAWING (DETAIL)

B45

Opposite: Full presentation drawing for a house.

Page 146: (Left) Partial view of lower floor plan with greenhouse and garden; (right) lower floor plan.

Page 147: Cross section.

Page 148: View of entrance.

Page 149: View of west facade.

CROSS SECTION

U/S ROOF 107'-6"

LIVING 100'-0"
DINING 98'-0"

ENTRANCE 94'-0"
LOWER FLOOR 90'-0"

VEGETABLES

GREEN HOUSE

UPPER FLOOR PLAN

NORTH

SITE AND LOWER FLOOR PLAN

1589

HOUSE FOR RAY & GRACE ROBINS
H.E. KUCKEIN ARCHITECT M.R.A.I.C.

98

APRIL

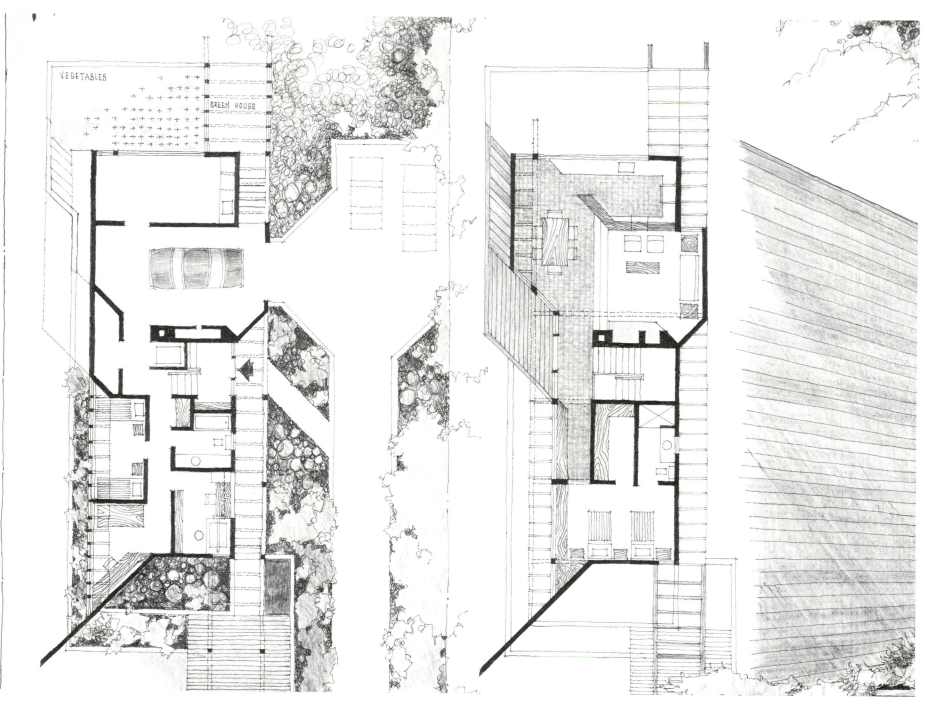

VEGETABLES

GREEN HOUSE

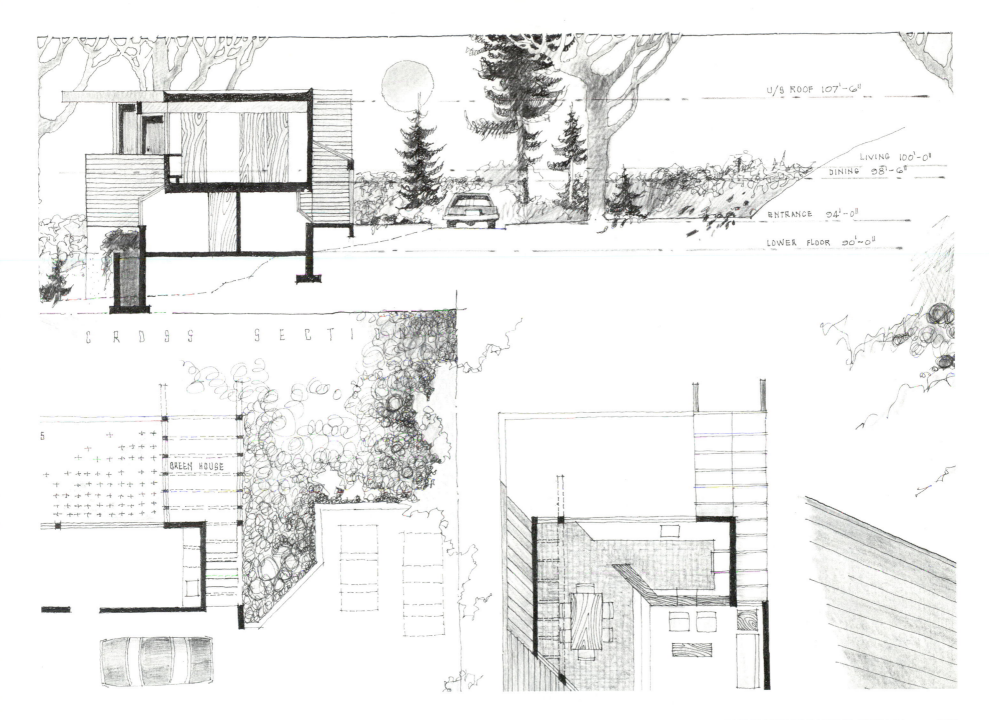

U/S ROOF 107'-6"

LIVING 100'-0"
DINING 98'-6"

ENTRANCE 94'-0"

LOWER FLOOR 90'-0"

CROSS SECTION

GREEN HOUSE

148   PRESENTATION DRAWING (DETAIL)

B46

Opposite: Proposal drawing for house near the ocean.

Page 152: Partial view of main floor living area.

Page 153: Site plan, showing sun angles.

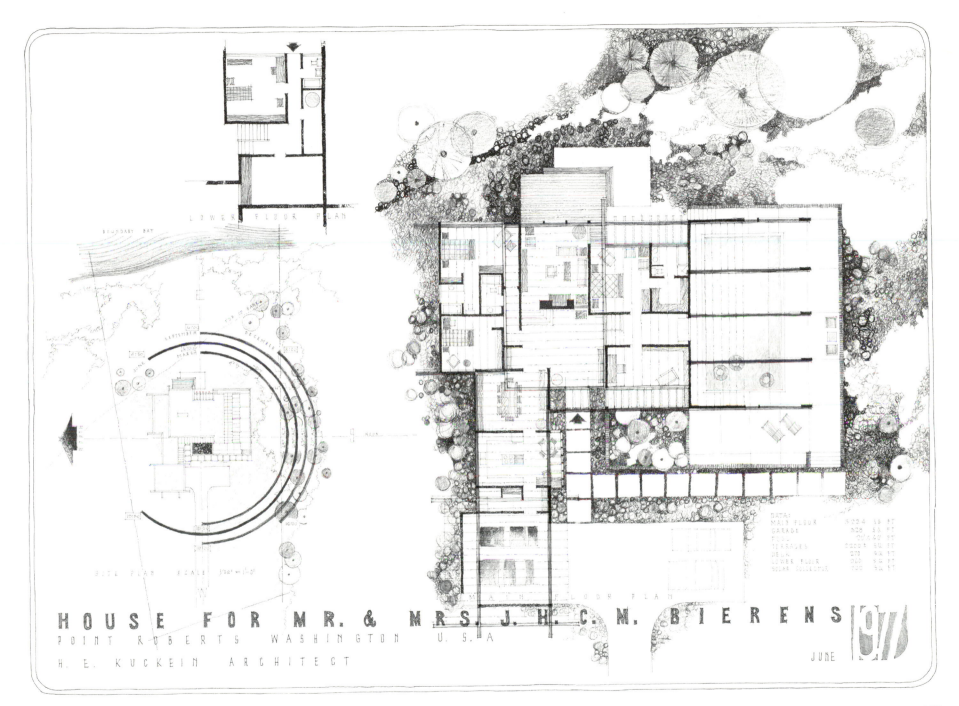

LOWER FLOOR PLAN

BOUNDARY BAY

SITE PLAN   SCALE 3/32" = 1'-0"

MAIN FLOOR PLAN

DATA:
MAIN FLOOR   3224 SQ. FT.
GARAGE   528 SQ. FT.
POOL   20440 SQ. FT.
TERRACES   2200 SQ. FT.
DECK   270 SQ. FT.
LOWER FLOOR   960 SQ. FT.
SOLAR COLLECTOR   700 SQ. FT.

HOUSE FOR MR. & MRS. J. H. C. M. BIERENS

POINT ROBERTS WASHINGTON U.S.A.

H. E. KUCKEIN ARCHITECT

JUNE 1977

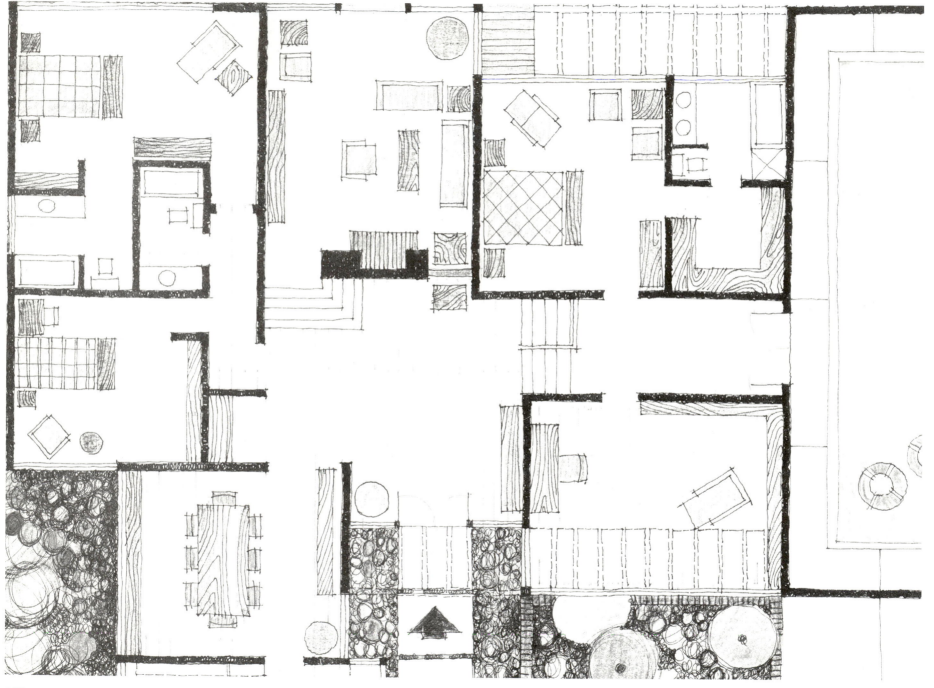

152   PRESENTATION DRAWING (DETAIL)

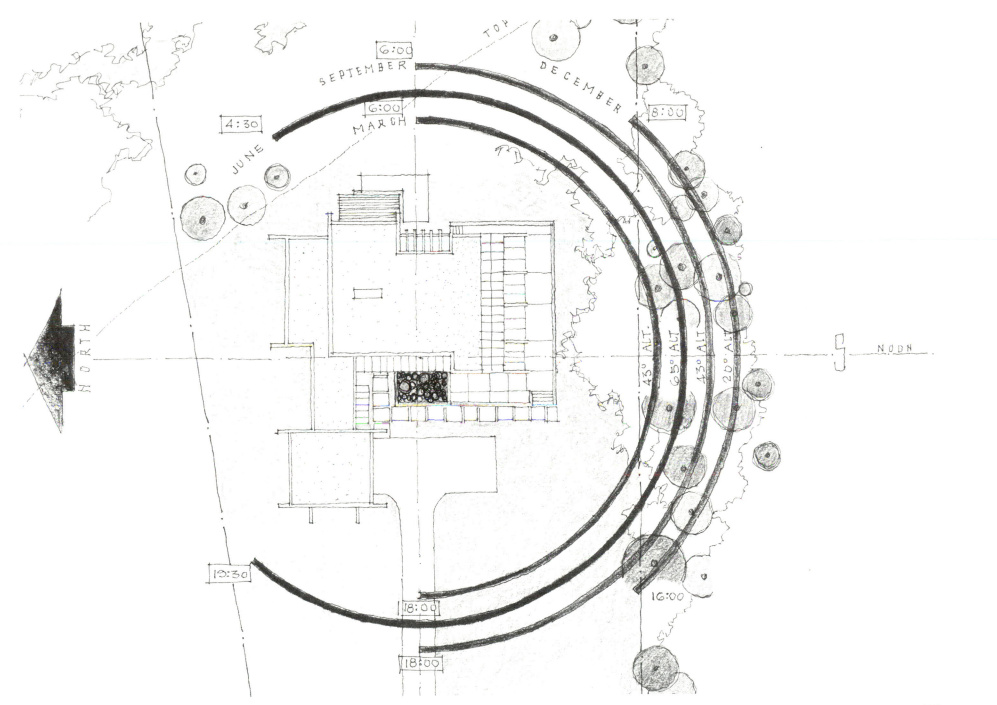

NORTH

JUNE 4:30
SEPTEMBER 6:00
MARCH 6:00
TOP
DECEMBER
8:00

NOON

43° ALT.
65° ALT.
43° ALT.
20° ALT.

19:30
18:00
18:00
16:00

B47

Opposite: Proposal drawing for a house near the ocean.

Page 156: View of main entrance.

Page 157: View of entrance court.

HOUSE FOR MR. & MRS. J. H. C. M. BIERENS

POINT ROBERTS   WASHINGTON   U.S.A.

H. E. KUGKEIN   ARCHITECT

EAST ELEVATION

VIEW OF MAIN ENTRANCE

JUNE 1971

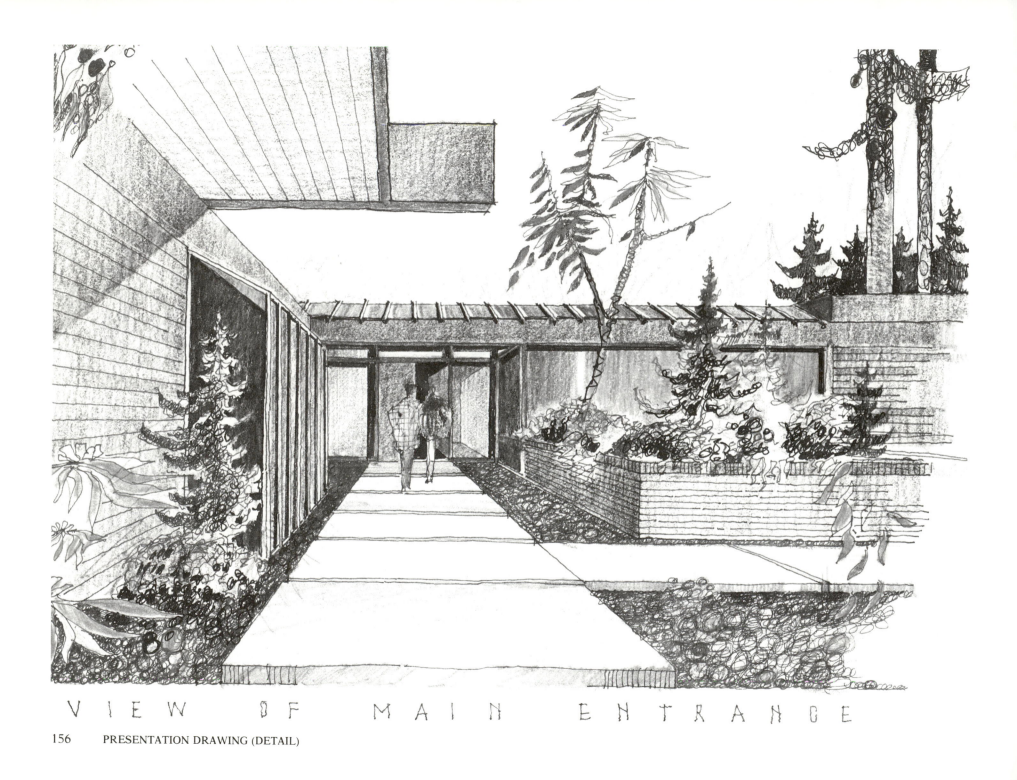

VIEW OF MAIN ENTRANCE

PRESENTATION DRAWING (DETAIL)

B48

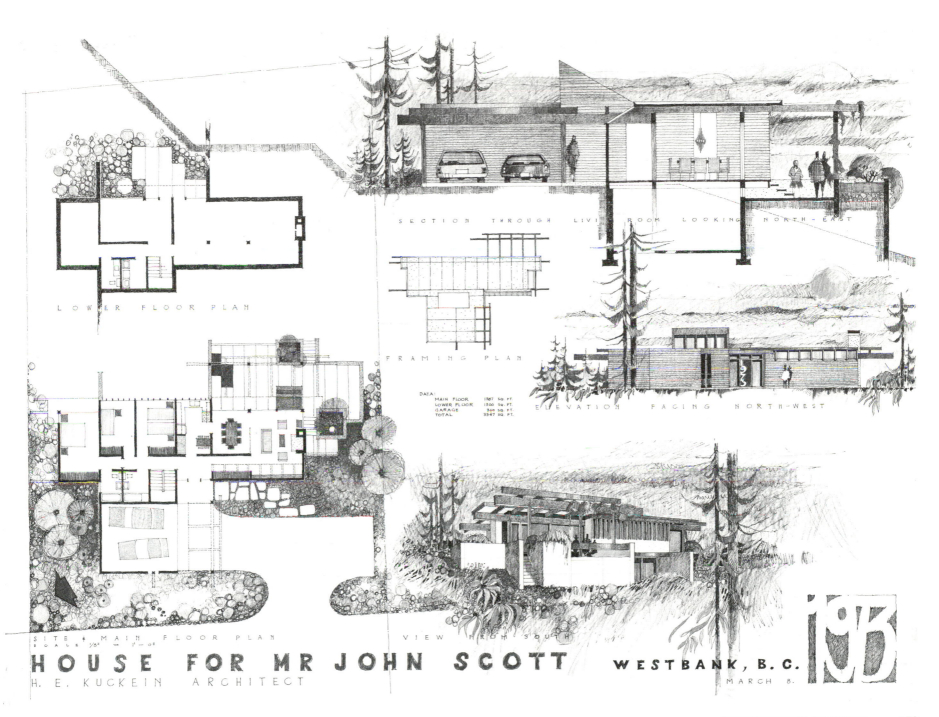

LOWER FLOOR PLAN

SECTION THROUGH LIVING ROOM LOOKING NORTH-EAST

FRAMING PLAN

DATA:
MAIN FLOOR 1387 SQ. FT.
LOWER FLOOR 1300 SQ. FT.
GARAGE 300 SQ. FT.
TOTAL 3347 SQ. FT.

ELEVATION FACING NORTH-WEST

SITE + MAIN FLOOR PLAN
SCALE 1/8" = 1'-0"

VIEW FROM SOUTH

HOUSE FOR MR JOHN SCOTT WESTBANK, B.C.
H. E. KUCKEIN ARCHITECT

MARCH 8.

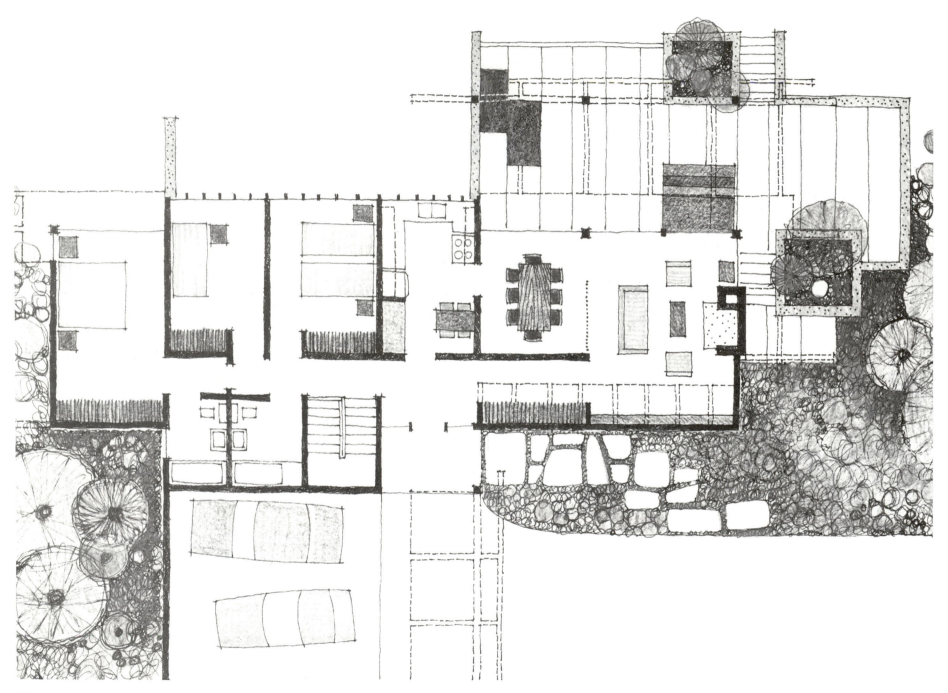

EW FROM SOUTH

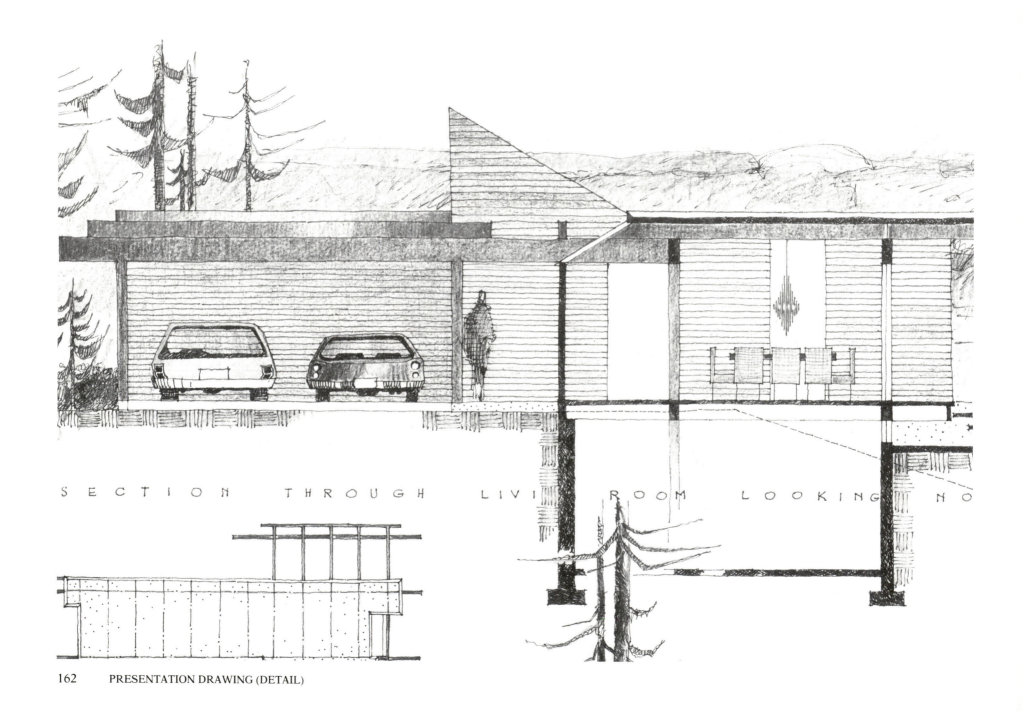

SECTION THROUGH LIVING ROOM LOOKING NO

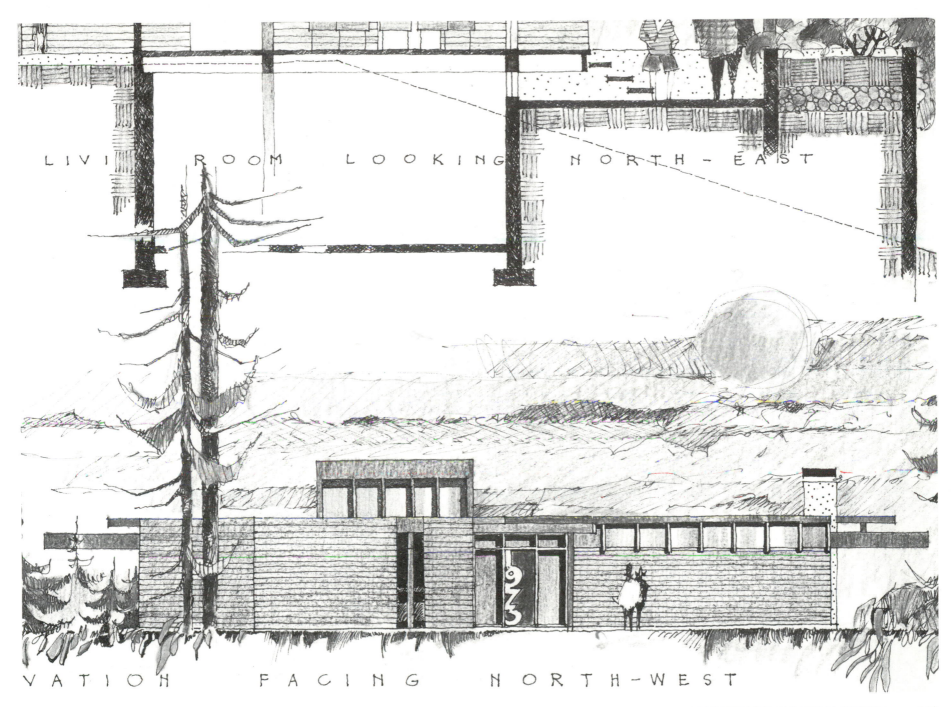

LIVI   ROOM   LOOKING   NORTH - EAST

VATION   FACING   NORTH-WEST

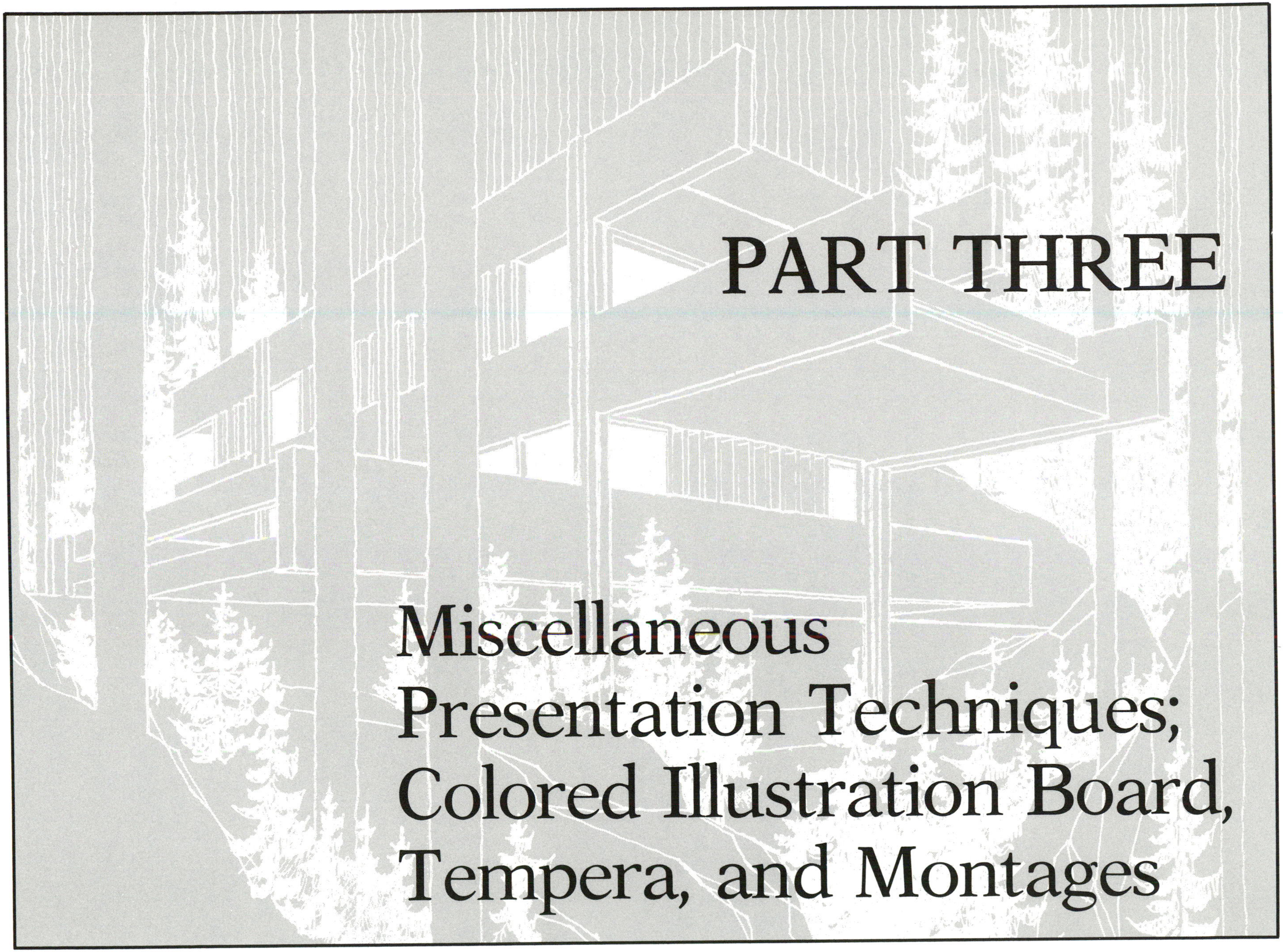

PART THREE

Miscellaneous
Presentation Techniques;
Colored Illustration Board,
Tempera, and Montages

In the preceding parts of this book we discussed the more conventional methods of representing objects. That information will suffice to give the interested student a vocabulary with which to work effectively. Another means of communicating in the graphic context, however, is what I call assemblage. It serves as a means of study for work to be presented to clients, and for graphics to be included in periodicals. The medium I am now describing is achieved by approaches that are simple, varied, and interesting, and the success of the work that is based on this medium will depend largely on the contents of your portfolio discussed earlier, which must contain illustrations, photographs, and clippings on a variety of subjects that are likely to become part of the work you are going to be doing. The illustrations in this chapter will give you a good idea of what I mean, and should allow you to get started at once.

If you prefer, you may study the presentation work in this book by beginning with this chapter. It will put you on an exciting path that will lead you quickly to professional looking graphic art; however, it appears in the final part of this book for good reasons! As stated before, the techniques discussed here are simple; in fact, they are so elementary that virtually everyone has at one time or another employed some of them in their lives, perhaps in projects undertaken at kindergarten or public school. To raise this part of graphic art to levels acceptable for inclusion in architectural work is, needless to say, a more demanding task, which requires of students an understanding of design and composition, a feeling for color, a sense for proportion, and, last but certainly not least, an appreciation of architecture.

The equipment and materials required to achieve fine results are limited yet flexible; that is to say, one may start with a small investment and build up an assortment of items required as expertise increases and as situations demand. The goal in most cases is to produce professional looking presentation work with a minimum of effort, often an essential and important factor in the operation of a design studio. A voluminous portfolio filled with the many elements that form part of this type of work will contribute greatly to the speedy and effective achievement of the desired results. Next, you should select various illustration boards of good quality and appropriate color and texture as they

Introduction

form the base to which the various graphic materials—whether paint or cut-outs—will be fastened and on which the mood of the final product frequently depends. A jar of good quality white tempera, three or four tubes of watercolor paint, a fine brush, a pair of scissors capable of cutting detailed configurations, and a fine, sharp cutting knife are the only equipment required, for it is assumed that at this stage of your development you already have the indispensable utensils such as pencils and pens and are now able to employ them with a measure of confidence. There are no set rules about which way to begin. Every situation seems to invite an approach unlike any other. Undoubtedly, as you evolve your own way of working, as you must, your approach will change. Also, you will find that your goal may be to produce graphic work that is simple and low key, or to develop an approach that will dramatize important qualities in your composition. With the required equipment at hand and your mind in a somewhat analytical state, let us discuss the illustrations included here for study.

C1

A muted green, finely textured illustration board formed the basis for the study of the proportions of this house. What is it that we want to feature or bring into focus as we begin to assemble the composition? The house is of frame construction, faced on the exterior with stucco, painted pure white. The setting is a lushly overgrown hilltop richly endowed with a variety of trees. Since the house can be seen mainly from the street, the presentation concentrates on the elevation facing it. The green background is suggestive of the setting. By adding a few deciduous and coniferous trees we can enhance this feeling. In contrast, the walls are stark white so as to indicate the appearance of the completed project. All elements were roughed in with pencil, followed by freehand ink work. The texture of the trees and left foreground was achieved by a circular motion with a fine ink pen. Wood surfaces in shade received a texture of horizontal and vertical lines in contrast to the remaining wood facing, which consists of carefully drawn vertical lines. Glass in shade occurs in black in order to give the required contrast and depth. Ink work thus far completed, the remaining wall surfaces were simply painted with white tempera, thinned to a consistency that makes it workable with a brush. The paint took only a few minutes to dry. Next, the white wall surface in shade was stippled with an ink pen. You should do this exercise before you go on as it will give you a feeling for the technique. Furthermore, you will learn to use tempera paint. Then you may wish to try your own composition in a similar manner.

C2

This is a study for a summer house to be located on a steep ravine overlooking the ocean. Without an accurate site survey at this stage, the configurations of the land mass can only be guessed at, and so a few simple lines are used merely to suggest the dramatic topography of the area. The muted orange of the illustration board, which unfortunately is not reproducible here, hints at summer, vacation, and fun. A few pines, the sky, and the water, which is indicated with a few vertical lines, complete the natural environment. As for the house, only the general mass is indicated; all materials and textures are left for further development. Highlights of white tempera complete this preliminary design study. The time required to produce it might be less than two hours.

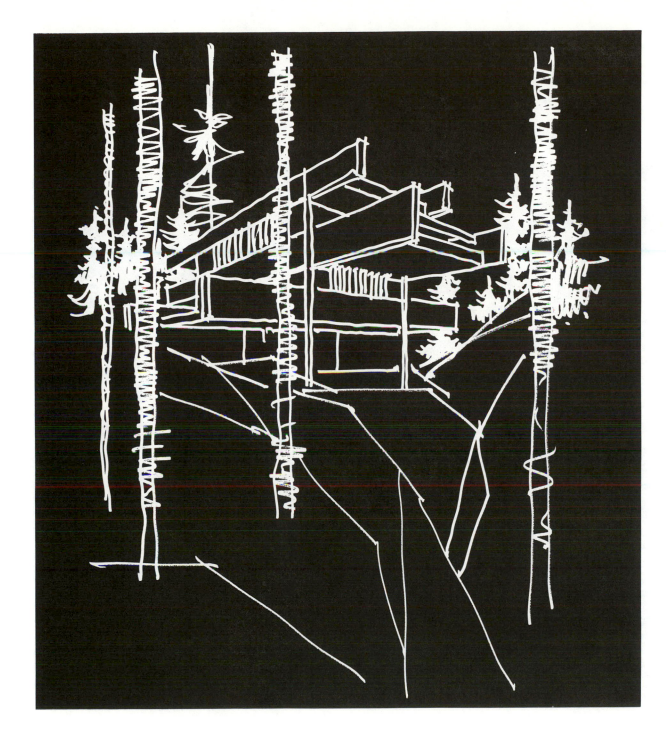

C3

This ink sketch put down in a few minutes of a project discussed in previous chapters is included here to demonstrate that quickly executed conceptional sketches may contain much information for a designer. Drawn at "thumbnail" size, they may be printed in reverse as in this illustration or greatly enlarged, resulting in exciting graphics. In any case, they are frequently the basis for and precede further development of a project.

C4

Here is another project that you are familiar with from having studied the previous lessons. Laid down in less than five minutes, it gives preliminary information with respect to proportion and character. The medium is the same as in C3.

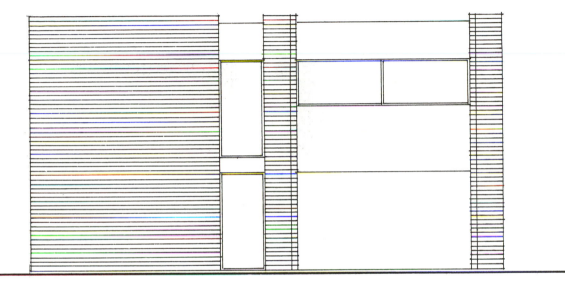

C5

The outline of the street elevation is from a project discussed earlier. Drawn with a fine ink pen and instruments on a drafting board, it provides information about its proportions, but it lacks interest. Let's see what can be done to create some vitality and reality in the drawing by adding cuttings from colored photographs and other material from our portfolio.

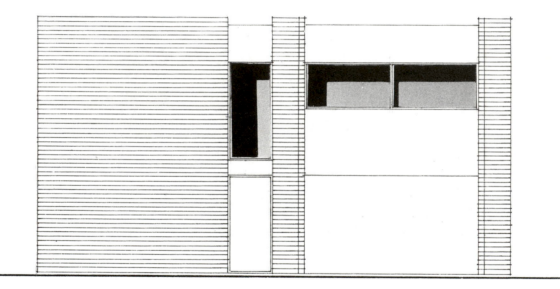

C6

*In the original drawing, blue paper approximating a sky color,
blackened with ink (to suggest the shadow cast on the window
panels), is cut to appropriate sizes and fastened with rubber cement,
as shown. Instantly a sense of reality enlivens this drawing.*

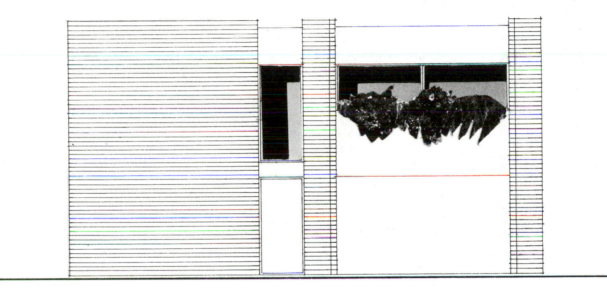

C7

Shrubbery and flowers cut from material in the portfolio are glued into the area of the flower box in front of the windows.

C8

*Now, let us assume that the structure is located on a lovely site
overlooking a lake and mountains. A color photograph of the site in
relative scale is cut to the perimeter of the house and fastened with
glue. A tree on the left stands ahead of it. In minutes the
uninteresting facade has been transformed; it now possesses depth
and reality.*

C9

The automobile in the right foreground and the figure are added to give scale, and thus further enhance the picture. One could go on, applying the brick and wood facing cut from photographs, but sometimes it's best to leave the work at a stage such as this. When you undertake this type of illustration work, simply snap a photograph in black and white or in color of the site on which the project is to be located, have it enlarged to an appropriate size, and follow the procedure used to prepare this illustration. Your portfolio should be filled with material that will give you quick access to the required entourage. A photo of your client in the illustration, or perhaps his dog, will contribute significantly by adding a sense of reality and humor.

C10

Another approach was used in the illustration of this house, which we discussed earlier. In the original drawing, ink work was applied freehand with a fine pen to muted light brown illustration board. The sky was indicated with horizontal lines, the spaces between them diminishing toward the horizon. The significant features of the project are the earth berms and the glass roof; thus they were the focus of attention in the application of tempera paint mixed with watercolor to appropriate tones of sky color and vegetation. The slight differentiation between glass panels adds reality. The earth berms to be covered with green ivy were stippled with an ink pen after the paint was dry. The low moon adds charm. In the original drawing, it is painted a bright ochre.

C11

This is a somewhat more complex illustration of a project discussed earlier in terms of the media employed. It is now drawn in ink, freehand, on a medium brown illustration board. Dark young pines contrast against the trunks of the mature trees, drawn without foliage. Sky "tone" is achieved by the even vertical ink lines, which give definition. The structure is emphasized by the addition of white tempera applied facing one direction to all surfaces of the house. A good brush will make this an easy task. Although high contrast is the key note of this presentation, a feeling of softness prevails.

RENDERING OF A VACATION HOUSE   179

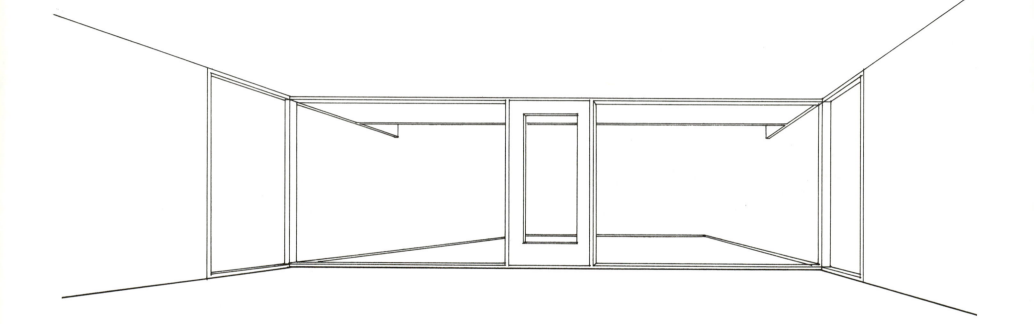

C12

This ink outline drawing in elementary one-point perspective depicts one of a number of living units for a resort to be located on a hill overlooking a lake. Several of these drawings were produced in an effort to arrive at the most satisfactory design solution. Photographs taken from several vantage points on the site permitted a careful study of the problem. The next illustration indicates the value of such an undertaking.

C13

One of the numerous photographs taken of the area is here cut into the window of one of the units. A few pots of geraniums from photographs in my portfolio give scale and color. Needless to say, this offers an appropriate method to study a design problem, and is very helpful indeed in communicating one's ideas to a client.

C14

As part of an urban housing project, it was necessary to give potential occupants an indication of the view to be expected from the suites. A simple one-point perspective was drawn in ink, as shown. It took perhaps no more than ten minutes to complete the drawing, but at this stage it conveys little. Let us see what can be accomplished by introducing some cutouts.

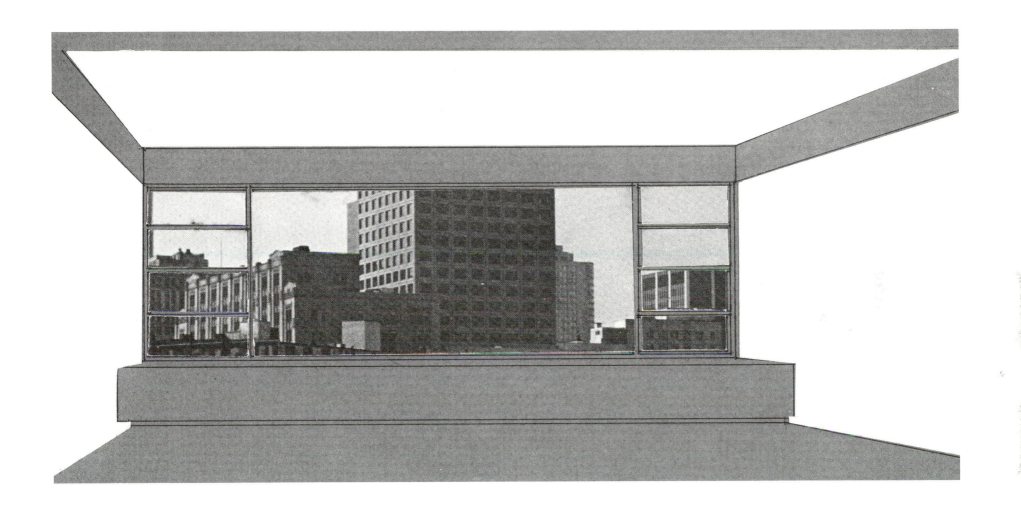

C15

Several photographs were taken with a telephoto lens from buildings in the area, enlarged to appropriate size, and these were cut and glued into the glazed areas of the window wall. One of several studies made is included here. Wall and ceiling areas of white paper add *reality. The entire assemblage took only a short amount of time yet contributed greatly in clarifying a situation. I hope that you will recognize the value of this simple method of architectural illustration. You will not regret becoming skilled in the use of this medium.*

AUTHOR'S NOTE

A book of instruction should be an inspiration to the student. With this objective in mind, I arranged the lessons in this book so they would allow those unfamiliar with the subject to start at the beginning and to progress as time and ability permit. Your progress through this book is not unlike that experienced by students who have spent time with me in a classroom or studio and on outdoor sketching trips. The teaching environment here, although informal, has been structured to enable you to rapidly and effectively develop a sound discipline, which I believe is an essential part of architectural drawing. The text has been kept brief throughout, and focuses attention on the various illustrations and the techniques employed to produce them. Learning a graphic vocabulary is an awkward experience even for the most ambitious and talented students. However, seeing progress, observing yourself become proficient and more at ease with each new lesson, will itself be inspiring as it will encourage you to undertake more difficult tasks. Whatever your ambitions, enjoy your drawing and draw with confidence. Your enjoyment will soon become evident and much delight will await you. My sincerest good wishes are with you.

The following materials were employed in the preparation of the illustrations contained in this book.

Graphite pencil leads: Faber-Castell 2H, F, 2B, 4B.

Ink pens: KOH-I-NOOR Rapidograph.

Technical fountain pens: Point sizes 3X0, 00, 2.

Ink: Pelikan, waterproof drawing ink.

Tempera paint: Pelikan graphic white.

Watercolor: Winsor & Newton, bright red, lemon yellow, cerulean blue.

Glue: Rubber cement.

Brush: Winsor & Newton, sable hair.

Eraser: Faber, Pink Pearl.

White illustration board: Hi-Art No. 62 Illustration Board.

Colored illustration board: Tweedweave cover. (assorted colors) by Curtis Paper Company.

Colored pencils: A.W. Faber, Castell Polychromos 9201 series
- Ochre 184
- Van Dyke Brown 176
- Light Blue 147
- Brown Ochre 182
- Raw Umber 180
- Orange 115
- Dark Blue 151
Eagle Prismacolor
- Olive Green 911
- Scarlet Red 922

Fixative: No. 1306 Krylon workable fixative. Atelier clear spray coating.

Cutting knife: X-acto.

MATERIALS

Notes

Notes

ACKNOWLEDGMENTS & CREDITS

All illustrations prepared by the author except the following:

Photograph A54: Williams Brothers, Photographers, Vancouver, B.C.

Illustration B30: Project for a resort. John H. Hanson, Architects, Vancouver, B.C.

Photograph B33: F. Lindner, Photographer, Vancouver, B.C.

Illustration B36: "805 Broadway," an office building. Vladimir Plavsic, Architects, Vancouver, B.C.